AN ARTFUL LIFE

Inspirational Stories and Essays for the Artist in Everyone

John P. Weiss

Copyright 2017 by John P. Weiss

ALL RIGHTS RESERVED

No portion of this book may be reproduced, stored in a retrieval system, or transmitted in any form or by any means—electronic, mechanical, photocopy, recording, scanning, or other—except for brief quotations in critical reviews or articles, with the prior written permission.

ISBN: 1546996907
ISBN 13: 9781546996903

Printed in the United States of America

The content in chapters 1–33 are reproduced here with the permission of the copyright holder, BoldBrush Technologies, LLC. This content may not be reproduced without the express permission of BoldBrush Technologies, LLC.

WHAT READERS ARE SAYING

"John, you know how to touch my soul. Great writing. Thanks."—Joseph

"Hearing from you is like hearing from a dear friend who is sharing yet another insight in this journey we call life. Thank you."—Susan

I look forward to your short stories, all with a very important art twist. You never fail to surprise."—Terry

"How can a sugarcoated story bring tears to my eyes? It did. Nice story, John."—Charles

"John, I am a new fan of you. I love your story writing, your art, and the person you are. You inspire me. I look forward to reading all your stories. Can't wait for more to enjoy."—Brenda

"I love your posts! They always strike a chord with what I'm doing or thinking. But you have such an engaging writing style that encapsulates so succinctly what has been mulling about in my brain's dark regions. Look forward to the next post!"—Janna

"Yes! You have the most engaging writing style, John!"—Carol

"This story brought tears to my eyes."—Walter

"Beautiful! John Weiss writes eloquently and informatively."—Meath

"This post was fantastic and exactly what I needed to read this morning. Thank you for your words."—David

This is lovely. Beautiful writing: it took me right back to my childhood. Thank you."—Ellen

For Nicole and Conner

ACKNOWLEDGMENTS

Living with an artist can be challenging. We're often distracted, forgetful, and lost in a world of endless creativity. Yet somehow, my wife Nicole puts up with me. My profound thanks and love. Ditto for my son, Conner, who is coming into his own as an amazing, creative soul.

Thanks to my mother, Patricia Weiss, for her endless love, support, and encouragement. And to my father, the late John B. Weiss, who is largely responsible for the man I am today. Not a day passes that I fail to think of you, Dad.

To my sister, Leslie Elizabeth, for inspiring me with our Sunday conversations over coffee. And to my in-laws, for your love and support: Richard, Nancy, Dave, Natalie, Antonio, Chris, Felicia, Ava, Danny, Michelle, Maya, and Arwen.

Thanks to my terrific editors, Carrie Turner (who invited me to write for *Fine Art Views*) and Angela Agosto, whose eagle eyes caught many a typo.

To Clint Watson, founder and CEO of FASO (Fine Art Studio Online), the premier website-creation tool and marketing system for fine artists. Clint has been most supportive of my creative efforts and cartooning, for which I am grateful. Also to FASO CMO Dave Geada and the fantastic support team at FASO, thanks for all your help and support.

John P. Weiss

And to everyone who has read my stories, commented on my blog posts, bought my artwork, and taken the time to finish this book. I am blessed to have fellow artists and readers who support my creative efforts. Best wishes to all in your artistic endeavors.

CONTENTS

What Readers Are Saying iii
Acknowledgments vii
Foreword by Clint Watson xiii

Chapter 1	A Phone Booth in the Woods	1
Chapter 2	How Your Creative Spirit Will Save You	5
Chapter 3	Why Freedom Is the Answer	9
Chapter 4	Memories Are Roses in Our Winter	12
Chapter 5	Seven Ways to Improve Your Artfulness	16
Chapter 6	Madam Painter	21
Chapter 7	This Is What Happens When You Become an Artist	25
Chapter 8	If You Want to Be an Artist, Understand Loneliness	30
Chapter 9	The Treasure Map	35
Chapter 10	How to Get Unstuck When You Feel Like Quitting	39
Chapter 11	Why Minimalism and Hope Make You Happy	43
Chapter 12	The Irish Gentleman	48
Chapter 13	I Meet Dead People Every Day	53
Chapter 14	No, It's Not Too Late	59

Chapter 15	How Your Heart Can Improve Your Art	64
Chapter 16	How to Avoid the Renaissance-Man Trap	68
Chapter 17	This Is How Old Trees Speak to Us	73
Chapter 18	This Much I Know Is True	78
Chapter 19	This Is How Abandoning the Herd Can Bring Success	84
Chapter 20	The Flower Thief	89
Chapter 21	Sins of the Father	95
Chapter 22	Washing Away the Dust of Everyday Life	100
Chapter 23	Why People Pay Good Money to Brand Themselves	105
Chapter 24	The Gift Wrapper	111
Chapter 25	Minimalism and the Art of Creative Success	117
Chapter 26	Birds of a Feather	123
Chapter 27	Why Comparison Is the Thief of Joy	128
Chapter 28	The Prisoner	133
Chapter 29	The Surprising Value of Anger	139
Chapter 30	Why I Steal Like a Thief and You Should Too	145
Chapter 31	The Overlooked Benefits of Ruthless Editing	151
Chapter 32	If You Want to Be a Full-Time Artist, Read This	156
Chapter 33	This Is Why Art Will Never Let You Down	162
Chapter 34	The Secret to a Happy Marriage	167
Chapter 35	The Power of Letting Go	170
Chapter 36	A Better Life Requires This	173
Chapter 37	Your Second Death and How to Transcend It	175
Chapter 38	The Most Important Quality to Look For in a Significant Other	178
Chapter 39	Why the Three Bs Can Ruin Your Life	180
Chapter 40	What Michelangelo Can Teach Us about Success	182
Chapter 41	Lessons on Love and Death from an Oak Tree	185
Chapter 42	Why You Need to Climb That Mountain	187

Chapter 43	How to Take Charge of Your Unhappiness	190
Chapter 44	Three Reasons Why Elegance Is Better than Winning	193
Chapter 45	How to Live a Better Life in Three Keys	198
Chapter 46	I Found My Way on the Day They Stopped My Heart	201
Chapter 47	How to Avoid Drowning in the Deep End of Life	205
Chapter 48	Embrace Constructive Criticism for a Better You	208
Chapter 49	Improve Your Art by Swimming More Laps	210
Chapter 50	If You Want to Soar, You Have to Leap	212
Chapter 51	The Life-Changing Benefits of Unpacking	215
Chapter 52	How the Love of a Cat Conquers All	218
Chapter 53	The Greenhouse	222
Chapter 54	Why You Should Deal with the Boulders before the Pebbles	226
Chapter 55	How to Improve Your Art and Productivity with Deep Work	229
Chapter 56	Postcard to Mary	232
Chapter 57	Do You Remember Who You Were?	234
Chapter 58	Love from Chubby Hubby	238
Chapter 59	The Art of Leaving Things Undone	243
Chapter 60	Want to Improve Your Art and Life? Embrace Solitude	246
Chapter 61	Why Autumn Is the Perfect Time to Let Things Go	249
Chapter 62	An Artist Is a World Trapped in a Person	252
Chapter 63	There Is a Way to Be Brave Again	254
Chapter 64	This Is How to Conjure Your Best Creative Self	257
Chapter 65	Why Grit Matters More than Gadgets	260
Chapter 66	We Waste a Lot of It	263
Chapter 67	The Morning Fox	265

Author's Note 269
Special Offer 270
About the Author 271

FOREWORD
by Clint Watson

There have been countless books, essays and blog posts written on the topic of "How to Sell Art." And while that is an important topic, it's been exhaustively explored. This book is *different*. It explores even more important ideas. You see, John P. Weiss is one of the precious few of us who is publicly exploring the vastly more important topics surrounding the emotional and human impacts of art. In other words, he's exploring the merits of living *An Artful Life*. Upon reading the first essay that John wrote for our online daily newsletter, *FineArtViews*, I knew that I had found a kindred soul and that his writings were something extremely special. John is a person who deeply understands the incredible power that art has to inspire people, to move people, to heal people, and to greatly improve people's lives.

In one of his essays, John shares the following Henry David Thoreau quote, "Most men lead lives of quiet desperation and go to the grave with their songs still in them." You, dear artist, are one of the blessed. You have the opportunity to defy the outcome of most men. You are blessed to know what your "song" is, and you are blessed to have the opportunity to let it out, in vibrant color, into this world, here and now. God has bestowed upon you the incredible gift to create art. And that gift affords you the opportunity to truly *Live* with a capital L. Because art improves the world, you have the privilege . . . and the *responsibility* to utilize your God-given gift. That includes both the responsibility *to create* your art, thus making *your* life better, as well as the responsibility *to share* your art with all of us, thus making *our* lives better. I've often written that sharing your art will change the world, and, even if your art only improves *your* world, then the undertaking is still worth it. But *inevitably*, while in the process of changing your own world, you *will* impact others and make this planet a better place for countless other lives.

While a few of us, myself included, have, for years, explored these themes in piecemeal fashion in our blog posts, websites and newsletters, the book you hold in your hands is a true treasure, and one that you will cherish. It is, in itself, a true work of art and a beautiful gift of creation from John that takes this important message to another level. Through moving, engaging, and entertaining stories, these essays explore the importance of art in improving the human condition with a clarity and power that is beyond *anything* I've ever personally written or read. So, as you devour John's stories, prepare to laugh, prepare to cry and, most of all, prepare to be moved to understand that *your art is far more important than even you probably realize*. Whether you're a seasoned pro, or a noble "weekend warrior", by the time you finish this book, you will be inspired like never before to stand before your easel and get on with the important work of making the world a better place for all of us.

To an artful life,
Clint Watson
Founder of BoldBrush and FASO

CHAPTER 1

A PHONE BOOTH IN THE WOODS

I had been hiking for a while in the back country, lugging a knapsack full of landscape-painting equipment. My pochade box, solvents, paints, panels, and the hope that inspiration would strike. The late November air was brisk and invigorating. The deer paths were narrow but led to a promising opening. A vista, just beyond the trees and brush.

I emerged from the woods to an open meadow of soft grass, grand views, and an inexplicable discovery. For there, disconnected from the world in a forgotten meadow, a lonely and weathered phone booth stood. I stared at its tired structure, covered in twigs and yesteryear's dust. And then, the phone rang.

Voices from the past
I looked around. Had I stumbled upon an elaborate joke? But there were no hidden cameras or grinning pranksters in the woods. Just me and this ringing vestige from the past.

I set down my pack and wrestled open the phone booth's folding glass door. Strange to be inside a phone booth in this age of smartphones and instant communication. I lifted the receiver and said, "Hello?" At first, static. But then I heard the distant sounds of holiday music, a doorbell ringing, and a dog barking.

It was so familiar, these mysterious sounds in the receiver. Next, I heard the creak of a door opening and a boy's voice. "Hey, Seth, come on in. Did you bring your sketchbook?"

I stood there in the phone booth, speechless. The voice on the line was me, when I was thirteen years old. The dog barking was Ebony, our family's small black poodle. Seth is my childhood friend.

Except I'm fifty-one years old. My buddy Seth is fifty-two. Ebony died decades ago. How could any of this be possible?

What would you say to yourself?
I listened intently and could hear my mother's voice in the background. "Dinner's in about an hour, boys, so don't disappear outside." My friend Seth said something about a toy snake he brought over to scare my sister with. Next there were footsteps. Then I heard my younger self say, "Hey, someone forgot to hang up the phone." There was a brief fumbling sound, followed by "Hello?"

"Uh, is this John?" I asked, unsure what to say.

"I'm Johnny. You probably want my dad. May I ask who's calling?"

I stood frozen. Dad passed away in 2004. How I longed to talk to him again. There was some static on the line. "Johnny, I'm an old relative calling long distance. Say, how's your artwork coming along? Are you still into that fantasy artist, Frank Frazetta?"

"Yeah, I have three Frazetta books now! Since it's getting close to Christmas, I asked Dad for my own oil-painting set. But he said it all depends on my school grades."

So many forgotten memories! I recalled that I had been struggling a bit in private school back then. Always drawing instead of studying. And my father kept telling me that art was fine, but I needed a stable career to rely on.

"Well, your dad's right, Johnny. I know Harker Academy can be tough, but hang in there. And your algebra teacher, Colonel Tuttle? I'm pretty sure you'll get a B in his class. In fact, you're gonna do just fine." My eyes were a little moist. I felt strange. So many emotions crashing down from the past.

"Okay, cool. Well, here's my dad." As I heard those words, I thought my heart would stop. But suddenly, clear as day, his strong baritone came on the line. "Hello?"

The gift of gratitude

I had to think fast. My father had been an administrative-law judge. I remembered that when I was thirteen, he was still recovering from a stress-related heart attack. He'd been emotionally down, unsure of his health and future.

"Judge Weiss, this is Father Patrick. You probably don't remember me, but I visited you while you were in recovery after your bypass surgery." It was a lie, but a pretty clever one, I thought.

"I'm sorry, Father, I don't recall your visit," my father said.

"That's fine, Judge. The hospital provided your phone number, and I just wanted to follow up." As I spoke, the connection started to break slightly.

"Well, thank you, Father, I'm feeling much better."

"Judge, when you were in recovery you spoke a bit in your sleep. If you'll indulge me, I just want to tell you. You're going to be fine and live a long life. Your wife, Pat, will always be cared for. Your daughter and son will both land solid careers. But your son, he'll always be an artist at heart." The static was starting to come back on the line.

"Well, thank you, Father. Very kind of you to say." My father was skeptical, but cordial.

"Oh, and, Judge, your family loves you more than you know. And they always will." There were tears in my eyes now, but I felt joy in the thought that I was able to express immense gratitude.

"I'm sorry, Father, what was your name again?" my father asked.

"John Patrick, Dad. It's John Patrick." And with that the dial tone disappeared. I hung up the receiver, exited the phone booth, and collapsed in the grass beside my painting gear. Emotionally exhausted and overwhelmed, I closed my eyes. When I awoke a bit later, the phone booth was gone, but a sort of peace washed over me.

Find your own phone booth
We don't have to stumble upon a miraculous phone booth in the woods to reach out to the ones we love. We just have to reach out. Through our art, our words, our actions, our forgiveness, and our love.

Take a moment to find your own phone booth in the woods. And when it rings, do yourself a favor and have the courage to pick up the receiver.

CHAPTER 2

HOW YOUR CREATIVE SPIRIT WILL SAVE YOU

It seems like yesterday that I held his hand and told him it was okay to let go. That we would all be fine. Our lives were set on a sure and promising trajectory, thanks to his years of love, sacrifice, and guidance.

The hospice nurse told me that hearing is often the last sense to go. I believed her because as I reminisced with my dying father, his eyebrows would raise occasionally. He seemed to acknowledge and understand each revisited memory. Unable to speak and cocooned in that protective coma, his mind could still access my words. Their meaning. And the difficult message that it was okay to cross over the veil.

The facade of immunity
Obituaries are instructive if we take the time to read them. They contain the full constellation of human experiences. From young love to marriage, work, family, legacy, and the final struggles of aging.

A few years before I lost my father, we strolled the cemetery where he had bought a plot. "Johnny, look at all these headstones. Each one is a story," he said to me. "So many lives. Marriages, mortgages, children raised. Promotions, demotions. Dreams met, others lost."

My father was an administrative-law judge. A historian, bibliophile, and polymath. In early adulthood I began to truly appreciate his wisdom and insights. That day in the cemetery he conveyed an important message. None of us are immune from death. What mattered was how we lived our lives.

I remember better when I paint

PBS recently aired a fascinating documentary about Alzheimer's and dementia patients. Specifically, how they come alive when given the opportunity to create art. As one expert in the video states, "The creative arts are an avenue to tap into a nonverbal, emotional place in a person." The documentary further explains that "people still have imaginations intact all the way to the very, very end of their progressive disease."

The documentary illustrates the awakening of one woman who seems permanently lost in the fog of dementia. And yet, with the patience of a young artist, the woman slowly emerges from her cognitive decline and begins to create art. She starts to express herself creatively. She unveils a deeper expression, beyond the parameters of superficial conversation.

Portal to the soul

In an essay titled "Why the Arts Are Key to Dementia Care," writer Anne Basting notes, "How can we stay connected and foster what has come to be called the 'personhood' of someone with dementia or Alzheimer's? The answer is: the arts. A symbolic and emotional communication system, the arts don't rely on linear memory and rational language. Rather, the arts engage our intuition and imagination. Their building blocks for expression are movement, gesture, words, patterns, sounds, color, rhythm, texture and smell—to name just a few. As access to rational language falters, a person's imagination can soar."

In another article titled "Art Therapy and Dementia—How Creativity Helps Unlock Alzheimer's Patients' Thoughts and Fears," the following observation is shared by Dr. Daniel Potts: "Art therapy is helpful for dementia and Alzheimer's patients because it enables an individual who is having trouble communicating to bypass the language problems they may be having and communicate and express themselves in a different way."

"It gives an individual a sense of accomplishment," added Potts. "They're losing their cognition, but art therapy gives them a way to create and get some satisfaction. It allows their true self to be expressed when it otherwise can't."

In essence, the mind may be faltering, but artistic expression miraculously remains. Perhaps the final portal to our souls.

Your creative spirit will save you
As creative artists we spend a lot of time anguishing over our art, success, recognition, and legacy. We fiddle with our websites, enlist social media, wrestle with our creative compulsions, and soldier on. We have little choice. Our creative expression must be released. At times our artistic efforts bring great satisfaction. On bad days, we experience deep frustration. Such is the path of an artist.

My father was a weekend oil painter. His full-time devotion was to the law, history, books, and intellectual pursuits. And yet I remember the cartoons he used to leave in my grade school lunch box. Those amusing caricatures, jokes, and notes of encouragement. I also cherish the oil paintings he left behind, hanging to this day in my home.

I like to think that in the twilight of my father's last days, beyond the logic of law and ordered thoughts, it was his creative spirit that comforted him. That my colorful recollections of summer and past vacations caused his eyebrows to dance. Perhaps that artful muse lay beside him, caressed his face, and said, "You have lived, loved, worked, and created things of beauty. Rest now."

I believe the greatest gift is our creative spirit. She dances with us, even in the throes of Alzheimer's and the fragility of old age. She will accompany us beyond the indignities of infirmity, to the ultimate mysteries of living and dying. It is our creative spirit, that gentle lifelong companion, who will save us in the end.

CHAPTER 3

WHY FREEDOM IS THE ANSWER

Have you ever noticed that everybody is searching for the answer? The solution to help us finally achieve the life we always dreamed of. The secret revealed that will untether us from the unpleasant trappings and mundane realities in our lives.

For many, wealth is perceived as the ultimate answer. And to some extent, money does make life easier. Being able to afford food, dental care, and a nice home brings a measure of peace. Yet there are plenty of affluent people who remain unhappy. So what's the answer?

Lives of quiet desperation
American author and poet Henry David Thoreau was way ahead of today's minimalist movement. Long before popular websites like ZenHabits.com and becomingminimalist.com, Thoreau had this to say: "Most men lead lives of quiet desperation and go to the grave with their songs still in them."

Thoreau's famous book, *Walden*, was an experiment with simple living and personal reflection. In a way, he went to Walden because he was searching, too. I suspect he studied the world around him and the natural rhythms of life. Work, raising a family, paying one's bills. He probably took to Walden on a spiritual quest to escape the petty things of society. To find something more.

How artist Rick Howell found the answer
A few years back, I discovered the paintings and website of Rick Howell. I liked his tonal landscapes and even bought his instructional DVD.

In a *Southwest Art* magazine article, Howell was asked why he left his investment business. Howell replied, "I had been painting since junior high school, and I always wanted to be a painter. But I didn't think you could make a living at it. One day I was driving back from one of my brokerage branches in Boulder. I was dressed in a suit and tie and the air conditioning was going. I suddenly looked over at the guy next to me, who was driving an old Jeep. He looked like he didn't have much, but he looked like he was enjoying life. In that moment I just realized that money wasn't my main goal in life. I just wanted to follow my dream—to paint. I thought, "If I am going to go for this, now is the time." Gauguin was also a stockbroker, and he quit about this same time in his life. He became successful, and I thought, "If he can do it, I can do it." I turned in my resignation two days later."

Shades of Henry David Thoreau
Rick Howell moved into a 150-year-old adobe home in Colorado and converted its largest room into a studio. He spent most of his time painting outdoors, even in the winter. Because he felt, "Plein air paintings have a raw honesty that one is not able to get from working from a photograph in the studio."

Howell was a private man, often shunning art openings. Clearly, he had found his answer. His purpose. His *Walden*. He found his freedom in painting.

Galleries encouraged Howell to push more color in his work, but that wasn't his style or vision. As friends on his website attest, Rick Howell was "...always true to himself."

Sadly, Rick Howell passed away in 2012. A remembrance on his website states, "We were not surprised to hear that Rick passed away from what they call an 'enlarged heart,' he was an immensely kind and generous man who took in lost dogs, fed stray cats and cared for most everyone who crossed his path."

Freedom is the answer

I grew up in a fairly affluent neighborhood, but everyone was still mortgaged to the hilt, driving leased BMW's and maxing out their credit cards. Folks were still having heart attacks and divorces. As the Dalai Lama points out, "We have bigger homes, but smaller families; more conveniences, but less time."

Freedom is the answer. Whether from an unfulfilling job, unhealthy relationship, or just too much stuff. Freedom is a real option in our lives, but it requires forethought and courage. It took courage for Rick Howell to leave his investment business, but it bought him years of painting bliss. His charitable soul and kindness to animals were no doubt a reflection of a man at peace.

Henry David Thoreau wrote, "I did not wish to live what was not life, living is so dear, nor did I wish to practice resignation, unless it was quite necessary." Dear reader, don't live a life of quiet desperation or resignation. Summon the courage and forethought, and then embrace freedom. Your *Walden* awaits you.

CHAPTER 4

MEMORIES ARE ROSES IN OUR WINTER

The old gentleman knew that more years were chasing him than remained. His beloved Betty had passed away last December. It was awful. He awoke that chilly winter morning and found her in his art studio, on the floor. A tea cup shattered beside her frail body. And in her left hand, his recent painting of daffodils. It comforted him immensely. That in her final moments, she had picked up his little flower painting. Betty loved the garden and especially daffodils.

"They don't ask anything of nobody. You just put them in the ground. In decent soil. Then let them do their thing." He could still hear her lyrical voice saying that.

"I love their brilliant yellow. They look like a cup and saucer. So uplifting. So full of promise and renewal, don't you think?" He smiled at the memory of that. "Yes, Betty, I do think you're right," he said to himself. "It's why I painted the daffodils for you."

The inevitable transition
Later that spring, he heard the familiar sound of his son's truck pull into the driveway. "Hey, Dad, sorry, I didn't call. Thought I'd

An Artful Life

check in on you." The old gentleman let his son in the front door. "Where's Carol and the kids?" he asked. "Oh, they're at the shopping mall. Carol said something about a new Coach purse." But the old gentleman knew it was a lie. Benevolent, but a lie nonetheless. No, his son had come for "the talk."

"It's just that with Mom gone now, there's no one to look after you, Dad. And besides, you've seen those apartments at Oak Street Villa. There's enough room for you to set up your art studio. It's a nice retirement community." His son meant well. But he wasn't old enough to understand the long shadow of grief that accompanies the loss of a spouse. Or the pain of facing the inevitable transition. Leaving the home you spent a lifetime in, only to descend into a community of the irrelevant and forgotten.

"Come on, Dad, it's not like that. You'll have company. You won't have to cook. You'll be closer to me, Carol, and the kids."

And so, with that, he looked at his son. "Okay, I guess it's time. Time for Croak Street Villa."

His son frowned. "No, Dad, Oak Street Villa, not Croak Street. That not even funny."

Memories are roses in our winter
The move went as well as expected. Going through Betty's old clothing and things was hard. But he was settled into the new apartment now, and his son was right. There was sufficient room for his art studio. Still, he missed Betty terribly. At night, she'd come to him in his dreams. They were young again and laughing. He mused about his artistic ambitions. She'd emerge, smiling, from the daffodils in her garden. But then he'd awake, to the solitude. At least he still had his art.

The staff at Oak Street Villa were kind enough and arranged for several of his pieces to be hung around the facility. Maria, one of the nurses, asked him about Betty once, and how he dealt with her loss. "I don't think I have dealt with it," he told her. "I just go to bed at night, hoping. Hoping that she'll come visit me." And then he said this: "Memories are roses in our winter. I read that in a George Will column once. Never forgot it. Because it's true. In the autumn of our lives, well, we still have our memories." Maria's eyes welled with tears when she heard that.

Who will be my Mendelssohn?
The old gentleman often joined the others in the dining hall. He was known around the place, due to his artwork. One old chap, a retired literature professor, had taken to calling him "Monet."

"Hey, Monet, I saw that new garden painting you did in the front lobby. Beautiful piece," said the professor.

"Well, my wife kept a beautiful garden. It reminds me of her." It was all the old gentleman could think to say.

The professor suggested he paint more pieces for the many halls and lobbies at Oak Street Villa. "What's the point?" the old man said. "No one is interested in an old man's flower paintings. People today like that modern stuff."

With that, the professor became quite serious and said, "Johann Sebastian Bach's music wasn't broadly appreciated until after his death, eighty years later. When another composer, Mendelssohn, played it all over Germany. Same with Thoreau. His Walden Pond wasn't embraced by the public until after his death. So, you just keep painting. You never know when or how your art will impact others."

The old gentleman just smiled and said, "Well, I don't know who my Mendelssohn will be."

The healing power of art
A few years crept by and the old gentleman did his best to paint, but arthritis and cataracts were his enemies now. His son and family would visit, but something inside of himself said it was time. He

dreamt that final night of a daffodil garden, and in the distance he saw her. Betty was smiling and waving to him. Beckoning.

In the weeks after his death, his son and family cleared out the apartment and said their good-byes to the staff. It was poignant for everyone.

A month later, another family arrived with their aging mother. She had lost her husband and was terribly afraid of change. She felt so very alone in this new place. The kind nurse, Maria, told her that a wonderful artist used to live in her apartment. But the old woman was still afraid. "Tell me your story," Maria asked. "What did you use to do?"

And the old woman said, "I raised my children while Carl, my husband, worked at the bank. Oh, and I gardened. Tulips, roses. And especially daffodils," said the old woman.

The second night in her new apartment, the old woman sipped some tea and continued unpacking. At one point she sat down and wept. Change was so hard. But then she clicked the light on in her closet. And noticed an object on the top shelf. Using a stool she reached up and slid out the small painting. She took it down into the light.

Gazing at it, she began to feel a sense of peace wash over her. "It's so beautiful," she thought. "This must be a sign. Maybe I'll be okay, after all."

The next day she visited the front desk and asked if there was a frame shop in town. "Why do you ask?" said the girl at the desk.

"Because I have the loveliest daffodil painting, and I want everyone to see how splendid it is."

CHAPTER 5

SEVEN WAYS TO IMPROVE YOUR ARTFULNESS

I am interested in art as a means of living a life; not as a means of making a living.

—Robert Henri

Many of you are probably familiar with the artist Robert Henri and his beloved book *The Art Spirit*. The back jacket of his book has this to say about him:

> Robert Henri (1865–1929) was an American artist, teacher, and an outspoken advocate of modernism in painting. He is best known for his leadership of the group of realist painters known as "The Eight," later termed the Ashcan School. Henri was a devotee of realism and the usage of everyday city life as subject matter. He taught at the Art Students League in New York from 1915–1928, and had a profound

influence upon early 20th century painters such as Stuart Davis, Rockwell Kent, and Edward Hopper.

Many years ago, when I transitioned from cartooning to landscape painting, I picked up *The Art Spirit*. I underlined various passages that spoke to me. But over time, having grown as an artist, the wisdom of Henri's words and insights became much greater. Every page had me saying, "Yes, exactly."

I believe that embracing an artful life is one of the most rewarding ways to live. There is great beauty in the world. Be it nature, art, literature, film, music, crafts, or whatever quickens your creative heart and soul. But learning to build more artfulness in your life requires some focus and intentionality. As Robert Henri put it, "If you are to make great art, it will be because you have become a deep thinker."

I have assembled seven ways to improve your artfulness. Adopting these strategies has definitely increased my artfulness and creative approach to everyday living. These tips are not the obvious things, like "paint more often" or "read poetry" or "buy flowers." Nope. These tips are deeper practices that, if adopted, will free you to embrace more artful living.

Become curious
It's not hard to fall into a rut. Work routines, the rhythms of family life, and responsibilities all have a way of scripting our days. As a result, little energy is left for curiosity. But we must fight this.

Consider the wisdom of Albert Einstein: "I have no special abilities; I am only passionately curious." Einstein no doubt had commitments and a busy schedule. But he entertained his curiosity. He asked questions like, "What if?" As artists and creatives, we should nurture our curiosity. By constantly asking questions and learning new things, we broaden our world view and stimulate the collision of ideas. All of which helps fuel our artfulness. One way to expand our curiosity: books.

Read books
Books have a distinct advantage over blogs and online sources. The advantage is that books are more closely edited and usually contain deeply thought-out content. Did you know that if you read just twenty pages a day, you'd be able to consume about thirty or more books per year?

Reading a broad array of books, both fiction and nonfiction, will expand your intellectual horizons and expose you to new ideas, places, people, and viewpoints. Our friend Robert Henri should weigh in here with his wisdom: "We read books. They make us think. It matters very little whether we agree with the books or not." He goes on to say, "If you are to make great art it will be because you have become a deep thinker."

Start journaling
I'm a big fan of journaling. It doesn't matter what approach you use. Some people like to chronicle their days, much like a diary. Others use journals to express free-form thinking. I use a combination of daily record and miscellaneous quotes, ideas, feelings, goals, and random sketches. Also, there's something about the physicality of pen and paper that promotes artfulness.

I find a free-form, unstructured approach unearths more personal truths. Much the way a dream at night reflects your subconscious hinting at a solution to a problem you're experiencing.

Try minimalism
I've found that an uncluttered life is conducive to greater artfulness and creativity. When we are not drowning in messiness and clutter, we can think better. Marie Kondo's best-selling book, *The*

Life Changing Magic of Tidying Up, taught us to ask one question about each of our possessions: "Does this bring me joy?" If the answer is "no," then sell it, donate it, or dump it.

Minimalism extends to your schedule and time management, too. It's about learning to diplomatically say no to things you don't want to do, in order to free up time for the things that are important. Like reading and journaling, for example!

Rediscover concentration
I follow a writer/blogger named Cal Newport. Cal's "about" page states: "Cal Newport is an Assistant Professor of computer science at Georgetown University who specializes in the theory of distributed algorithms. He previously earned his Ph.D. from MIT in 2009 and graduated from Dartmouth College in 2004. In addition to his academic work, Newport is a writer who focuses on contrarian, evidence-based advice for building a successful and fulfilling life in school and after graduation." So, basically, Cal's pretty smart.

Cal just wrote a new book, titled *Deep Work*. It's about the ability to focus without distraction on a cognitively demanding task. Let's face it; in this day and age of social media and texting, most of us are marinating in superficiality. Yes, those Facebook animal videos are cute. Those one-line inspirational quotes are cool. But if you want to get to the next level with your art, you have to go deep. And that requires concentration. I've found that reading books strengthens my focus and concentration. I also try to eliminate all distractions when painting or writing.

Find more grace
There's so much ugliness, violence, and anger in the world. It's like the wolf is always at our door, salivating and waiting to pounce. The best way to counter all of this is grace. I think of grace as more than just elegance, attractive movement, or divine sanctification. I

equate grace in my life to a positive, personal poise and forgiving heart.

I read once that "anger is a hot coal in your hand. You can throw it at someone you're angry with, but you still burn your hand." Yes, anger (when properly channeled) can motivate you to accomplish things. Like the obese man who is angry at all the cruel, fat jokes. He uses his anger to work out and change his life. That's fine. But more often than not, people use anger for retribution and cruelty. Perhaps they find some satisfaction, but often their anger eats away at their humanity. If you want to improve your artfulness, learn to forgive more and find grace in your life.

Develop emotional maturity
Emotionally mature people are honest self-evaluators. In other words, they don't buy into their own cow manure. I've worked with people who always blame everyone else for their problems. And I've worked with people who take personal responsibility for their lives. I have found the latter to be much more refreshing to work with. And I've found them, on balance, to be happier people.

Emotionally mature people don't dwell on what they can't change. They don't waste time blaming. They find their away around roadblocks and problems. They constantly strive to improve themselves and share credit. If you work on your emotional maturity, you'll find you spend less time on negativity and playing the martyr. Which leaves a lot more time for creativity, artfulness, and positive pursuits.

We started with Robert Henri, so let's end with him: "An artist has got to get acquainted with himself just as much as he can. It is no easy job, for it is not a present-day habit of humanity." Henri also noted, "Find out what is really important to you. Then sing your song."

I hope the above seven tips improve your artfulness and help you to sing your song.

CHAPTER 6

MADAM PAINTER

Edward was an awkward boy and he knew it. Nature had not blessed him with striking features. Chubby, short, and freckled, he struggled to fit in at school. His protruding ears and pronounced overbite didn't help matters, nor the fact his father was an alcoholic. His mother loved him dearly, but she was gone a lot. She had to work at the grocery store, because her husband spent more time in local dive bars than the odd jobs he'd occasionally pick up.

"Hey, freak boy, what's in your lunch bag?" Edward knew the voice well. As he turned around, the school bully, Brent, grabbed the lunch bag from Edward and opened it. "Ah, look what we have here! Peanut butter and jelly." Brent shook it out of the bag and let it fall to the dirt. "Wait, here's a bag of M&M's. Cool! Guess I'll take this and let you live." Brent shoved Edward down and tossed the crumpled bag at him.

Edward never told his mother about Brent or the other mean kids at school. He tended to keep to himself and retreat into his imagination. He also loved the library, where he could read about other places and people. And the library was safe. But eventually school would get out, and he'd have to walk home.

One day, as he slid past the park fence on his route home, he noticed an old woman along the edge of the grass. Her clothing was tattered, and she wore a beanie cap. Beside her was a shopping cart with black, plastic bags. Edward was curious. In front of her was a small tripod and some sort of box. He knew to avoid strangers but could tell she was older. She looked kind.

"Hi." It was all Edward thought to say.

"Hello, young man." She smiled.

"What are you doing?" he asked.

"I'm trying to paint those trees over there. Aren't they lovely?"

Edward could see now that she was holding some paint brushes, and her box held a small canvas board and had paints inside it. He asked about the box, and she told him it was a pochade box.

"May I watch you paint?" Edward asked, setting his backpack down.

"Certainly you may. But only if you help me."

"I don't know how to paint."

"Your heart knows how to paint. You just need to let the rest of you catch up."

She handed him a brush and adjusted her tripod to lower the pochade box. He asked what her name was, and she said, simply, "Madam Painter."

A friendship was born. Each day after school, Edward would traverse the park and look for the old woman. Most days she was there, and the two would paint.

He began to learn about shapes, values, and color. She showed him how to sketch and simplify his drawings. And they'd talk. He told her about his dad.

"Your father loves you, Edward. But sometimes men get lost in themselves. Maybe they're sad, or someone hurt them long ago." She looked in his eyes.

"People hurt me, too. Like Brent." And he told her about the school bully. How mean the other kids could be because he looked funny.

"You look fine, Edward. Children can be cruel. If there's one thing I want you to know, it's that love and kindness are the most powerful things in the world. Love and kindness. Don't ever forget that, even when you're angry at the world." And then she hugged him.

After that day, Edward never saw the old woman again. He continued to walk through the park and search for her, but she was gone. Like a guardian angel, she had come into his life when he needed a friend and then vanished.

He continued to grow up. One Christmas his mother surprised him with a beautiful French easel. It was used but functional. Later, in high school he would meet a few students who liked art. He found some friends. His mom got a better job, and he got braces for his teeth. His dad surprised him one birthday with a set of oil paints. His way of atoning for the many times his drinking let Edward down.

Edward's art progressed, and he won a scholarship to a fine art college. Below his senior picture in the year book, his dedication read, "Thanks Mom, Dad, and Madam Painter."

Time marched forward. Edward's father eventually passed on, and his mother retired to a comfortable apartment. Edward's art career took off, and he became quite famous, successful, and well known in his home town. He married and had two children.

One day his daughter came home from school with a flier. The school had organized a fund-raiser for a student fighting leukemia. "Her name's Susie and she's real sick, Daddy. Can we help?" Edward picked up his daughter and said, "Of course, sweet heart. An old woman once taught me that the most important things in life are love and kindness. I'll donate a painting."

The night of the school benefit-auction it seemed most of the town turned out. Edward's painting attracted collectors from New York and a bidding war ensued. The painting sold for a small fortune and everyone applauded and cheered. The principal tearfully thanked Edward and asked if she could introduce him to Susie's parents. "Of course," Edward said. So they crossed the school auditorium and the principal said, "Edward, this is Susie's mother, Barbara. And this is her father, Brent."

Brent. He'd age, his hair thinned, and his eyes had softened a bit. No doubt life, and now his little girl's illness, had siphoned the childhood meanness out of him.

Brent's wife thanked Edward for his generosity. For helping their little girl. "I'm happy to help," Edward said. And then Brent stepped forward. He looked sadly into Edward's eyes. Then he put his arms around Edward, hugged him tightly and wept.

CHAPTER 7

THIS IS WHAT HAPPENS WHEN YOU BECOME AN ARTIST

Art holds fast when all else is lost.

—*German proverb*

Several years ago I found myself in Idaho, taking an intensive workshop with Scott Christensen. I was relatively new to landscape painting. Almost all the other participants were accomplished painters. With each outdoor excursion, it became painfully obvious that I was bringing up the rear of my class.

While the others quickly set up their portable easels and began painting, I was busy fiddling. Adjusting my Open Box M and squeezing out colors. Often, by the time I got my act together, it was time to pack up and head to a new location. Talk about demoralizing.

As luck would have it, Scott Christensen was much more than a phenomenal painter. He was a percipient instructor with that rare ability to figure out just what you and your art needed to improve. And for me, it was a dose of C. S. Lewis.

Comparison is the thief of joy

I'm fond of Teddy Roosevelt's famous line, "Comparison is the thief of joy." Its wisdom lies in the celebration of individuality against the futility of "keeping up with the Joneses."

Most of us have heroes and people we want to be like. Which is fine, up to a point. More accomplished individuals can inspire us to be better. To achieve more. But sooner or later, we must come to terms with who we are. Our assets and shortcomings. And from there we must assemble the scaffolds that build the authentic person we long to be.

Unfortunately, I was woefully unprepared to look inward at that first Christensen workshop. All I could do was fixate on my novice status.

As a recently appointed chief of police, I had reached the zenith of my law-enforcement profession. I was still marinating in the satisfaction of reaching the top 1 percent in my field. The select few who made it to the "top cop" position. Conversely, as a relatively new landscape painter, I was among the novices and less experienced. Still figuring out values and edges and how to set up my darn pochade box.

Scott Christensen was no doubt amused by this earnest but struggling cop artist. I think he sensed my frustration and desire to be further along. To be part of the select group of "more accomplished" painters.

One night Scott handed me a copy of a speech given by the novelist and lay theologian C. S. Lewis. The title of the speech was "The Inner Ring." Later that night, back in my cabin, I pulled out the speech and devoured every word.

War and Peace and the unwritten system

C. S. Lewis was a professor of medieval and Renaissance literature at Cambridge University and a fellow of Magdalene College, Cambridge. He is best known for his popular Narnia fantasy book series. "The Inner Ring" was his Memorial Lecture at King's College, University of London, in 1944.

C. S. Lewis opens his speech with a few lines from Tolstoy's *War and Peace*. He refers to a character named Boris, who figures out that within the official military hierarchy, there exists an "unwritten system," where true power resides.

This unwritten system doesn't exist in any military manual or company rule book. As C. S. Lewis states, "You discover gradually, in almost indefinable ways, that it (the unwritten system) exists and that you are outside it; and then later, perhaps, you are inside it."

C. S. Lewis's "The Inner Ring" warns us about our desire to join this inner ring: "As long as you are governed by that desire you will never get what you want. You are trying to peel an onion: if you succeed there will be nothing left. Until you conquer the fear of being an outsider, an outsider you will remain."

Friendship trumps the Inner Ring
Most of us want to be part of the "in" crowd. The cool people who are up on everything and "in the know." The first kids to get selected to join the team, as opposed to the dregs that are left over.

Except it's all a lie. It's transitory and short lived. It belies the greater truth that self-worth and human dignity trump station and status.

Listen to C. S. Lewis here as he explicates further: "Once the first novelty is worn off, the members of this circle will be no more interesting than your old friends. Why should they be? You were not looking for virtue or kindness or loyalty or humor or learning or wit or any of the things that can really be enjoyed. You merely wanted to be 'in.' And that is a pleasure that cannot last. As soon as your new associates have been staled to you by custom, you will be looking for another Ring. The rainbow's end will still be ahead of you. The old ring will now be only the drab background for your endeavor to enter the new one."

Ouch. I guess this longing to be part of the "in" group ain't all it's cracked up to be. And to be honest, once I became a police chief, the novelty of being a "community leader" quickly wore off.

So, if joining the inner circle doesn't promise happiness and fulfillment, what does? According to C. S. Lewis, the answer is true friendship. As C. S. Lewis goes on to say about friendship, "Aristotle placed it among the virtues. It causes perhaps half of all the happiness in the world, and no Inner Ring can ever have it."

Become a craftsman and conquer the fear of being an outsider
Alone that night in my Idaho cabin, reading C. S. Lewis's words, I began to recognize my folly. I was so busy feeling dejected about my "novice painter" status, I was missing out on the joy of the journey.

C. S. Lewis urges us to abandon this quest for the Inner Ring. He argues that if we break it, "a surprising result will follow. If in your working hours you make the work your end, you will presently find yourself all unawares inside the only circle in your profession that really matters. You will be one of the sound craftsmen, and other sound craftsmen will know it. This group of craftsmen will by no means coincide with the Inner Ring or the Important People in the Know."

In other words, go about your artwork. Listen to your internal spirit. Sure, learn from others. But stay true to the craftsman you are. Enjoy the journey you're on. As C. S. Lewis urges, "And if in your spare time you consort simply with the people you like, you will again find that you have come unawares to the real inside: that you are indeed snug and safe at the centre of something which, seen from without, would look exactly like an Inner Ring."

Thanks to Scott Christensen sharing C. S. Lewis's "Inner Ring" speech with me, I learned that it's okay to be the beginner. The novice on the "outside" trying to find my way.

Because in reality, we make our own "inner rings" by staying true to ourselves and our artistic sensibilities. In time, other craftsmen and artists will be drawn to our authenticity and sincerity. From there, true friendships blossom and a deep peace settles into our soul. And, dear reader, this is what happens when you become an artist.

CHAPTER 8

IF YOU WANT TO BE AN ARTIST, UNDERSTAND LONELINESS

The happiest of all lives is a busy solitude

—*Voltaire*

Author Kent Haruf wrote his novels in a prefabricated shed in the backyard of his home in Salida, Colorado. Which seems fitting for this examination of art and loneliness.

Haruf's last novel before his death was titled *Our Souls at Night*. This splendid, spare story is set in the plains of eastern Colorado in a small town. It tells the tale of Addie Moore (a widow) and Louis Waters (a widower). Living in a small town, both knew one another's spouses before their deaths.

One day Addie shows up at Louis's house and the following conversation ensues (Haruf conveyed conversation without the use of quotation marks).

> I wonder if you would consider coming to my house sometimes to sleep with me.

What? How do you mean?

I mean we're both alone. We've been by ourselves for too long. For years. I'm lonely. I think you might be too. I wonder if you would come and sleep in the night with me. And talk.

He stared at her, watching her, curious now, cautious.

You don't say anything. Have I taken your breath away? she said.

I guess you have.

I'm not talking about sex.

I wondered.

No, not sex. I'm not looking at it that way. I think I've lost any sexual impulse a long time ago. I'm talking about getting through the night. And lying warm in bed, companionably.

Wisdom from a Canadian artist

Canadian artist Robert Genn was famous for his twice weekly letters. He sent them, via e-mail, to a legion of subscribers who enjoyed his insights and wisdom on creative issues, art and life in general.

Genn weighed in once on the topic of loneliness. He wrote, "The art of effective aloneness includes the understanding that solitude is necessary for the creative gain." Genn quoted the self-improvement guru Bruce Barton, who said, "Most progress comes out of loneliness."

Robert Genn noted that many art students are immersed in the collaborative energy of school and classroom interactions. Such students enjoy the social connectivity of art clubs and related activities. But then they graduate.

As Genn wisely notes, "Companionship, for many of us, takes the form of a spouse or significant other. Generational relationships are also particularly rewarding—father-son, grandmother-granddaughter, that sort of thing. Professional associations, occasional clubs, informal gatherings, crit groups and coffee klatches can further the illusion we are not doing this on our own. 'We're born alone, we live alone, we die alone,' said Orson Welles. 'Only through our love and friendship can we create the illusion, for the moment, that we're not alone.'"

Robert Genn understood that if you want to be an artist, you better understand loneliness. Because like it or not, a good deal of painting, writing, sculpting, music, and such comes down to independent effort.

Late nights of sustained creation. Early morning epiphanies. Private frustrations and repetitive rituals. Long stretches of weekends and canvas time where you are deep in the thick of it. Navigating the whispers of inspiration, personal expression, and tortured execution. This is a big part of what it means to be an artist.

Loneliness is about connection, not proximity
Author Olivia Laing was on NPR a while back to talk with host Terry Gross about her new novel, *The Lonely City: Adventures in the Art of Being Alone*. Olivia's novel explores the lives of painter Edward Hopper, pop-artist Andy Warhol, photographer David Wojnarowicz, and the "outsider" painter Henry Darger.

Olivia's own journey includes moving to New York with a man she fell in love with. Only to have the relationship fall apart and Olivia to find herself "alone" in a new city. It is here that she discovers one can be surrounded by people but still be alone. Loneliness is about connection, not proximity.

It is the painter Henry Darger who is perhaps the most fascinating loner in Olivia's book. Darger worked for fifty-four years as a hospital janitor and rented a bedroom where each night he would paint. After his death over three hundred paintings were discovered.

The paintings were not without controversy, as many portrayed violence toward children. Still, his work has been vigorously collected. Which begs the question: Is loneliness a prerequisite for great art?

From oversocialization to solitude

In my own life, I am immersed in a constant onslaught of interaction and public exposure. My day job as a police chief requires regular communication with the public, coworkers, politicians, vendors, and more. It's challenging, rewarding, and exhausting. Exhausting because at heart I am an introvert, most happy in the solitude of my home.

My best creative work seems to flow late at night or early in the morning. When no one is around and I am free to access my deepest, artistic compulsions. For me, a degree of loneliness and solitude amplifies my creative juices and results in some of my best work. It seems I require abject quiet and no disruptions to tap into the deepest veins of creativity.

I suspect I'm not alone. I've met many a creative soul, from writers to painters. A good number of them seem to crave this same undisturbed serenity. Where they can be alone and conjure the best of their artful manifestations.

Yes, some enjoy the conviviality of plein air groups and art associations. But probe deeper and you'll find that many long for those quiet times of independent work. When they can listen to their muse and produce authentic, original work.

Living simply and paying attention

At one point in Kent Haruf's novel *Our Souls at Night*, Addie tells Louis, "I just want to live simply and pay attention to what's happening each day. And come sleep with you at night." And at another point: "I do love this physical world. I love this physical life with you. And the air and the country. The backyard, the gravel in the back alley. The grass. The cool nights. Lying in bed talking with you in the dark."

In many ways I think Addie's approach to life is a good prescription for artists. To live simply and pay attention to what's happening each day. Also, a good deal of painters, photographers, and writers can relate to the charms of this "physical world," with its backyards, gravel, grass, and cool nights. These are the places and things that inform many a creative work.

Like Addie and Louis, we all crave some degree of companionship and human interaction. But many artists also require a measure of solitude. Perhaps even loneliness. To harvest the deepest of our creative proclivities and innermost expressions.

Maybe that's why artists like Edward Hopper, Andy Warhol, and the reclusive Henry Darger lived the way they did. Whether existing in a sort of subterranean way or hiding in the plain sight of celebrity, they carried a kind of loneliness within them. And today's aspirational artists should take note and consider whether they can tolerate this dance with loneliness.

CHAPTER 9

THE TREASURE MAP

I'd been hiking for an hour in the arid landscape of Patagonia when I came upon an old cabin. It appeared to be a little guesthouse. A well-worn dirt path traced from the cabin to a large home in the distance. Just then, a grizzled looking man spoke to me from the cabin window.

"Can I help ya?"

"Uh, yeah. Sorry. Kind of got lost. I'm visiting friends in town." With that I set my backpack down. The old man opened the weathered cabin door and ambled out.

"Visitors sometimes get turned around out here. Or maybe it's the spirits. The woods and rocks. They have their ways," he said, drawing on a Camel cigarette. Then he coughed. A smoker's cough. Harsh and rattling with phlegm.

"Is this your place?" I asked.

"Nope. The whole spread belongs to Bob and Carole. They let me stay here. To write. Artists need their patrons, by God." His voice was gravel and silt. His face and hands were tan, wrinkled, and as worn as an old leather bag.

"Come inside, son. Have something cold to drink. I'll draw you a little map to find your way back to town." He exhaled, the smoke trailing as he turned toward the cabin.

"Much obliged," I said. Walking inside the cabin, I noticed shelves of books and a small writing desk with notepads and journals strewn about.

If you want different results, become a different person
He told me his name was Jim and that he divided his time between Montana and Arizona. I was unfamiliar with his work, but apparently he was a writer of some acclaim. I told him I was a landscape painter. I slid a few canvas panels out of my backpack to show him.

"Nice work. You've captured a bit of the dryness and solitude here," he said.

"Well, thanks. I'm in a few galleries but sales are tough. Honestly, I came to Arizona to explore some new landscape themes. Maybe figure out why my art's not selling better. My friends were kind enough to put me up."

"Tell you what," Jim said, "You give me one of them landscapes of yours, and I'll give you some advice. What do you say?" He smiled and took another drag on his cigarette.

"What the heck, why not," I said. With that he surveyed a few of my studies and selected one.

"I like this one; it captures the arid feel around here," Jim said. And then he pulled his chair close, squinted, and began.

"Son, if you want different results, you need to become a different person."

"Come again," I said.

"People always talk about finding themselves, but what they should be doing is creating themselves. Experimenting, changing things up." He looked around the cabin. "When I quit my job years ago as an accountant, I began writing with a computer. The early stuff was okay, but I realized I relied too much on the Internet. And on copying other writers I liked. I wasn't capturing enough truth. My truth."

Jim pointed at his writing desk. "I don't use a laptop to write. I do it longhand. My editor hates it, but the work is more organic. More honest. The long walks with the dogs help, too. Honestly, the problem with all those Internet gurus dispensing advice is that one size doesn't fit all. What works for you may not for me."

Jim held up a ballpoint pen. "This is all I need, and some paper. You can read, troll the Internet, and travel. But then you got to shut all that out. Tap the truth inside you. Become the person you need to be to create the work that's inside you."

You have to pay your debts

I looked around the spare cabin. Lots of books, a writing desk. "Why do you come here to work? I mean, I hear what you're saying about the solitude. But it sounds like you're successful enough to afford your own place."

"Because you have to pay your debts," Jim said. "Bob and Carole helped me when I was starting out. They're literary agents, and they took a gamble on an unknown writer from Montana. So I come and stay for a few months. Do readings in town at the bookshop they own." Jim flicked his cigarette in an ashtray, looked down, and said, "You got to pay your debts. It's not always easy or pretty. But it's how you can get up each day and look in the mirror. You can't become the best version of yourself until you pay your debts. Maybe even learn to forgive yourself for past mistakes."

Improve your art by letting go

The sun was starting to hang low, and I knew I had to get back. But somehow this old writer in a cabin touched me. So much wisdom. So I asked him, "Jim, you've had a look at my art. What can I do to sell more?"

"You'll find your way to that answer," Jim said, "but one thing that might help is learning to let go."

"What do you mean?" I asked.

"Well, we all start out by learning the basics. Then we try to emulate our idols. It's natural, really. We look at what works for others and chase that. Except it seldom works. We have to find the courage to let go of all that. When we do, we start to listen to what's really inside of us. All the greats reached that place. Where they tapped into their own brilliant authenticity."

I smiled at the truth of what Jim just said.

"You're a tonalist painter," Jim noted. "But I see a touch of Russell Chatham in your work. Maybe a bit of George Inness, too."

I dropped my head. He nailed it. Two of my favorite painters.

"Don't feel bad. I used to think I disguised my affection for Hemingway. Until my editor called me on it. Which was good. Because it got me past that. Helped me dig deeper. When I did, my work started to take off."

The treasure map
I thanked Jim for his hospitality and promised to check out his books. We shook hands, and armed with his little map drawing, I made my way back to town.

A few years passed and I'd read some of Jim's splendid novels. I adopted his advice, and my paintings indeed began to improve and sell well. Jim's wisdom literally changed my life. And then one day my wife found me sobbing. I had just read that Jim passed away. She held me, without saying a word.

The next day, my wife took the little map Jim had drawn and had it framed. Beneath the frame she added an inscription: "Jim's treasure map." I loved her for that.

The map hangs to this day in the studio cabin I built in the woods. Where I go to commune with the spirits of nature, let go, and remember the old man who gave me the map to a better future.

CHAPTER 10

HOW TO GET UNSTUCK WHEN YOU FEEL LIKE QUITTING

Think back to where it all began. Maybe you were a kid who fell in love with drawing? Or perhaps you were the one in grade school who cherished books and writing? Some of you might have been in a high school rock band, with dreams of stardom.

Creative people have different disciplines and origins, but they share one important ingredient. Artistic passion. That fire inside of you that consumes a lot of your time, energy, and dreams.

Like a faithful friend, your art is always there for you. Your own private world where time stands still. Where you are free to plumb the depths of creativity. Where the joy of personal expression rejuvenates and satisfies your need to create art.

If you think back to where it all began, you might conjure a time when everything was simpler. Back then it was just you and your art. Most of your audience was relegated to your parents, family, and friends.

Unfortunately, the march to time means that nothing stays the same. Careers, relationships, responsibilities, finances, and more conspire against your art. What's worse, the evolving landscape of social media, blogs, newsletters, and technology may overwhelm you. How can you possibly keep up and compete?

And that's when you first hear that frightened, defeated inner voice, whispering sadly, "What's the point? Maybe I should just quit."

When ambition gives way to despair
This is a tough topic because no one can predict every outcome. There are examples in life of people who weathered endless hardships in the pursuit of their goals. Abraham Lincoln comes to mind. What would America be like had he thrown in the towel and gone back to being a country lawyer?

Conversely, others give up on one path and find their true calling elsewhere. Consider Andrea Bocelli. He got a law degree at the University of Pisa. At age thirty he was working as a lawyer and moonlighting as a piano bar singer. But four years later, he quit his law practice to become a full-time singer. And now he's famous.

Some folks never give up on their dream and eventually succeed. Others make the decision to give up on one dream and pivot to a new dream, where they find success. Still others, sadly, lose their ambition and slide into despair.

If you're the one on the precipice looking down into that abyss of despair, do me a favor. Sit down for a moment. Take a deep breath, and examine the following six considerations to help get you unstuck.

Six considerations before you quit
First, go back to your origins. Why did you begin in the first place? Chances are because of the sheer joy. As a little boy, the first thing I drew were birds. I quickly discovered the joy of a blank page to sketch on.

Even now, at fifty-one years old, the blank page calls to me. So many possibilities! Instead of worrying about getting more likes on

Facebook or growing your newsletter subscribers, reconnect with the simple joy of your art. For many of us, we'll continue making art regardless of any fame or the lack thereof. Don't let delusions of grandeur rob you of the simple joy of self-expression.

Second, join the club! The reality is that most of us won't become famous or rich with our art. And that's okay. Really. Here's why: I have a beautiful Scott L. Christensen painting in my studio. I also have a lovely Kevin Courter painting in my living room. Beautiful pieces. But the paintings that bring me the most joy are the ones that my father did.

Dad was a full-time judge and weekend painter. Each piece of his that hangs in my house teleports me back to him. Back to my childhood home and the laughter and our silly poodle and the smell of turpentine where Dad painted. Each one of my dad's paintings shared a piece of his soul. To me, they're priceless. Before you quit your passion, consider what you may be denying the ones you love.

Third, I encourage you to punch insecurity in the face! I don't know about you, but I'm done with insecurity. Why do we cater to it, anyway? We all know that successful people feel fear and uncertainty too, but then they step into the fray anyway. We should too.

Fourth, get comfortable with experimentation. Everyone talks these days like they have all the answers. Like they have all the solutions. Increasingly, I'm beginning to think it's all a crap shoot. So rather than listening to some online guru or know it all, just dive in and try different stuff.

If "doing what you've always done gets what you've always got," then shake things up. Try new effects with a palette knife. If you adore color but your work's not selling, try going tonal. Maybe add some abstraction to that photorealistic piece. A little modification, tweaks, and changeups to your art could open new horizons. What a shame it would be to quit, when the answer for you was just around the corner.

Fifth, call for backup. Sorry, but I stole some lingo from my day job as a cop. Whenever we think we're in trouble or need help, cops call for backup. Having an experienced officer to watch your back and assist you on a call is golden. Artists and creatives can do the same thing. Enlist the instruction, support, and guidance of another artist. Be it art school, workshops, plein air clubs, or favorite online blogger, there are fellow creatives out there just like you. People who have been where you are and can offer a guiding hand and a bit of sympathy. An experienced artist just might help you find your problem and lead you back from the abyss.

Sixth, remember the Romans. After all, Rome wasn't built in a day. Improving your work takes serious time and effort. There will be plateaus, breakthroughs, and moments of despair. Some of the biggest names in art have traveled down the same path. Many stayed true to their art and weren't discovered until after their deaths. They just kept creating. Hopefully because of the simple joy it brings.

Is it ever okay to give up? Of course. Blind persistence and unachievable goals can bury you. The key is to not buy into your own cow manure. Get a broad array of opinions, rather than family and friends who will all say they love your work. Bottom line, does the work bring you joy? Even if you're terrible but happy in your art, then carry on unapologetically.

Author Anna Quindlen has this to say on the matter: "The thing that is really hard, and really amazing, is giving up on being perfect and beginning the work of becoming yourself."

Be yourself. Rediscover the original joy that your art brought you. Before you started worrying about selling and websites and recognition. Someday your work may bring awards. Or it might end up in your child's home, or a friend's. Every time they gaze at your art, it will bring a smile. And in this way, the spirit of your creative soul will live on.

CHAPTER 11

WHY MINIMALISM AND HOPE MAKE YOU HAPPY

This December I'll be leaving a good job to paint and write full-time. My work as a police chief pays well and includes excellent benefits. If money and security were top considerations, I'd put in another five years and max out my pension. But I can't.

Despite my pride and gratitude for having served in such a proud profession, the siren song of art and personal expression is too strong. For over twenty-six years, I suppressed the artist within in order to serve my community and wrestle with the dark underbelly of society. The suicides, traffic accidents, battered spouses, abandoned children, homeless, addicted, and mentally ill.

Not that there haven't been grand moments, too. People helped, exhilarating calls, projects realized, lives saved. Still, it's time to leave. Time for this accidental police chief to fulfill a childhood longing to become a professional artist.

The decision to go for it was hastened by three disparate people: my father, George Clooney, and Joshua Becker. Sharing their stories might help you get where you want to go in life, too.

Here comes the judge

My father was thirteen years older than my mom. He was already in his early forties when I came along. Dad was in labor relations back then but decided to go to law school at night. Despite being ill with a bad flu, he passed the state bar the first time. Eventually, he became an administrative-law judge for the California Public Utilities Commission.

When I was thirteen years old, he suffered a heart attack right in front of us in the living room. I held his hand while my mother phoned for help. I remember him looking at me and saying, "Keep a stiff upper lip, son." Dad was a stoic, of German stock.

Thankfully, Dad survived his heart attack and returned to the court room. He remained on the bench until his eventual retirement at the age of seventy-nine.

Unfortunately, his retirement was short. The fog of dementia sifted into his mind and later, renal failure. He was dead at eighty-two years of age.

I loved my father dearly and knew he worked into old age to provide a better life for his family. But his work required long commutes. We saw him briefly in the evenings and weekends. I often wondered if the added money and security were worth it. I resolved to have a longer retirement for myself someday.

How heavy is your backpack?

Years ago I watched the terrific movie *Up in the Air* starring George Clooney. Clooney plays Ryan Bingham, a guy whom companies use to fire people. Bingham spends a great deal of time flying around to different job sites to break the bad news to unlucky employees. As a side gig, Bingham is also a motivational speaker. He books speeches and walks on stage with a backpack, which he sets down on a table. What follows is the beginning of Bingham's speech:

> How much does your life weigh? Imagine for a second that you're carrying a backpack. I want you to feel the straps on

your shoulders. Feel 'em? Now I want you to pack it with all the stuff that you have in your life. You start with the little things. The things on shelves and in drawers, the knick-knacks, the collectibles. Feel the weight as that adds up. Then you start adding larger stuff, clothes, table-top appliances, lamps, linens, your TV. The backpack should be getting pretty heavy now. And you go bigger. Your couch, bed, your kitchen table. Stuff it all in there. Your car, get it in there. Your home, whether it's a studio apartment or a two-bedroom house. I want you to stuff it all into that backpack. Now try to walk. It's kind of hard, isn't it? This is what we do to ourselves on a daily basis. We weigh ourselves down until we can't even move. And make no mistake, moving is living.

Of course, it's too simplistic to use a backpack as an analogy for our lives. But I never forgot that scene. I never forgot the idea of "less." That all of us are surrounded by a lot of stuff and people and commitments and stress. Could there be a solution. A better way?

The more of less
There's a blogger and writer whom I've been following for some time now. As the inside jacket of his new book *The More of Less* states, "Joshua Becker is the founder and editor of Becoming Minimalist, a website that inspires millions around the world to own fewer possessions and find greater fulfillment in life."

On Memorial Day, 2008, Joshua Becker was busy cleaning out his cluttered garage. A chance conversation happened with his neighbor, who mentioned that her daughter was a minimalist. She added, "She keeps telling me I don't need to own all this stuff." That comment was the lodestar for Becker and would set him on a path to becoming a leading voice in today's minimalism and simplicity movement.

Becker and his wife sold, donated, and discarded over 60 percent of what they owned. In exchange they found a life of more freedom, contentment, and time to pursue their passions.

Becker defines minimalism as "the intentional promotion of the things we most value and the removal of anything that distracts us from them." Decluttering our homes, art studios, and lives leaves more room for living. My wife and I have started doing this. We're unconcerned with keeping up with the Joneses and want to simplify. To have more quality time and less stress. Becoming more minimalist has made me happier and more hopeful.

An emotion we need more of
The *Wall Street Journal* ran a fascinating article, titled "An Emotion We Need More Of." Hope is a very important ingredient in our mental and physical well-being. As the article states, "People who have a higher level of hope have healthier habits: They sleep and exercise more, eat more healthy foods and practice safer sex. They also have fewer colds, less hypertension and diabetes, are more likely to survive cancer and have less depression."

Apparently the crucial component of hope is "agency." This means that hopeful people aren't just optimistic; they actually have a strategy to achieve what they hope for and the motivation to implement their plans.

Hope requires several qualities, which include trust/connection to others, feeling strong/capable, having people who validate your strengths, spirituality or a belief in something bigger than yourself, and a survival belief that you'll find your way.

The good news is that hopefulness can be developed or improved in yourself. You can't control feeling hopeless, but you can control your response to it. How? Create a meditation for hope by writing down inspiring quotes and saving inspiring images. As the article states, "The abstract imagery will reach into the right hemisphere of your brain, which focuses on emotions, relationships and images."

Writing exercises also help as well as developing several goals rather than just one. That way, "If the goals in one area fail, the whole ship doesn't sink." Catching negative thoughts and then countering them with things you should be thankful for will minimize a sense of hopelessness.

This is how we succeed
Decluttering your home and areas of your life will go a long way to finding more happiness. Developing a more hopeful outlook will broaden your happiness. So why not empty that backpack and develop more hope? I'm sure it will improve both your art and life.

Perhaps Ralph Waldo Emerson should close this article with the best advice of all:

> To laugh often and much; to win the respect of intelligent people and the affection of children; to earn the appreciation of honest critics and endure the betrayal of false friends; to appreciate beauty; to find the best in others; to leave the world a bit better whether by a healthy child, a garden patch or a redeemed social condition; to know that one life has breathed easier because you have lived. This is to have succeeded.

CHAPTER 12

THE IRISH GENTLEMAN

Karen flew into the Dublin airport with only one carry-on bag and the hope that two weeks in Ireland would untangle her creative funk and heavy heart. Her friends back home asked, "Why Ireland?" She told them that her mother was half Irish and she always wanted to visit the old country. But that was only half true.

When Karen was a little girl, her Irish grandmother gave her an old 1910 book of poems and faerie drawings by Paddy O'Flannigan. Her grandmother said she had known the artist and that the book was magical and brought good luck. The drawings and watercolors in the book delighted Karen, and she used to spend hours copying them. Before long, Karen knew she wanted to become an artist. She went on to get a fine art degree and found employment as a staff artist for Hallmark.

Designing greeting cards broadened her artistic abilities, but soon marriage and children derailed her work. She stayed home to raise her two girls, while her husband Doug worked long hours in the law firm. The girls later graduated high school and went off to college. Karen finally had the time to take up her art again, crafting detailed ink and watercolor pieces.

Calm before the storm

Karen had entered her drawings and watercolors in local art competitions and won a few ribbons. Her years at Hallmark fetched an income, but she always dreamed of becoming a fine artist. She was thinking about creating a website for her artwork, but one night Doug said this: "Honey, your drawings are detailed and well done, but, I dunno. Don't you think more vibrant color and a modern look would make them more marketable?"

"A more modern look?" Karen asked. "Do you mean, more abstract?"

"Yeah, I guess so. Just not so old-fashioned looking. People aren't into that," Doug said. With that, her heart sank. Funny, how sometimes loved ones can wound the deepest.

Karen began to question her artwork and sought instruction at the local community college. She tried her hand at an expressionist painting class, but the work she produced felt awkward, inauthentic, and ugly. Around this time, she also noticed Doug was working late quite a bit. He claimed the law partners had assigned him an impossible case.

In reality, the impossible case was named Fiona, an attractive new attorney who joined the firm. By the end of the year, Doug came clean about the affair, and most of their subsequent divorce was amicable.

When she told her daughters that she needed a break and was thinking about a visit to Ireland to clear her head, they encouraged her to go. "It will be good for you, Mom. You deserve to be happy again," her youngest said.

Breakdown in County Clare

The Park House hotel in Galway was welcoming, and the local pubs and surrounding streets were vibrant and lively. Music seemed to be everywhere. Buskers on the walkways and singing within the pubs. Still, Karen felt restive and rented a car to visit the famed Cliffs of Moher. Traveling away from town, she took in the rolling green hills, stone fences, and errant sheep wandering about the countryside. So peaceful and serene.

Her GPS blurted directions in an Irish accent. She ventured into County Clare where the roads narrowed, and civilization seemed more remote. And then it happened. A sputter sound from the engine, followed by a lurch. Driving on the left side of the road with a left-handed stick shift had been difficult enough. But now her engine began smoking, and she was stalled in a grass turnout.

The Irish Gentleman

Thankfully, Karen's mobile phone worked, and she phoned the Park House hotel. Karen described the roadway and area where she broke down. The hotel reassured her they would send someone, but it would probably take an hour or two. "Well, isn't this just my life?" Karen thought. She grabbed her little sketchbook and decided to kill time and stroll to a nearby ring of trees.

Much to her surprise, she heard the faint sound of an accordion from within the thicket of trees. Edging closer, she worked her way up the circular mound that encased a few dozen trees and tall grass. There, seated beneath a tree, was an elderly Irish gentleman playing an accordion.

"Well, hello there, lass," he said to her. "Are you lost, my dear?" He had rosy cheeks, a shock of white hair and a glint in his eye, but his manner was kind and gentle.

"No, my car broke down, so I'm sort of stuck here until the hotel sends someone," Karen said.

"Perhaps you're not stuck, my dear. Sometimes the wee ones invite you. After all, you're standing in a faerie circle. You'll find them around these parts. Some are even government protected. Farmers work around them because it's bad luck to disturb the faerie circles. Some say it's bad luck to sit in them, but I like to take my chances." The old gentleman smiled as he pulled a smoking pipe out of his little leather bag.

"I've always loved Irish folklore. Compared to today's world it's just so…"

But before she could finish, the old gentleman said, "…comforting?"

Karen smiled. "Yes, comforting." She sat down, across from him. He puffed a moment on his pipe, looked out beyond her, and then spoke.

"My dear, there was a time when life was simpler. Before this modern world with its noise, computers, commotion, rudeness, and artifice. But when you leave Dublin and Galway and the cities, and venture into the country, we're still here. The aging but happy faces. With our simple kitchens, living rooms, wall hangings, cupboards, thatch roof cottages, and wool sweaters. We are here with our sheep and stories and earthen rings. We still sing in our pubs and tend to the land."

"And I love that about Ireland. I feel like I can breathe here," Karen said.

"That's because people here are better connected to the things that matter. By the way, is that a sketchbook you have there, lass?" And with that Karen told him her story. Her childhood faerie book. The Hallmark years. Doug's hurtful remark about her art. The divorce. All of it.

When she finished, the old Irish gentleman stood up and smiled. "Listen to your heart, my dear. Even the wee ones here will tell you. Reconnect to the things that matter. As we like to say, 'may you be in heaven a half hour before the devil knows you're dead.' You deserve to escape the bad and start living again, my lass."

With that, Karen began to sob gently and the old gentleman hugged her. "There, there, lass. You'll be fine now." He held her gently, patting her back. He smelled of fresh grass and morning dew.

Just then Karen heard the approach of a car down the road. It was one of the hotel porters. She ran out into the narrow roadway and waved to the driver, who pulled in behind her stalled rental car. "Am I glad to see you. I was worried I'd be stranded out here all night!" Karen said.

The porter smiled and said, "No bother, I'll have you back straight away."

Karen thanked him and said, "Well, at least I had company," and she turned to point to the old gentleman. But he was nowhere to be found.

Healing at the Cliffs of Moher

The Cliffs of Moher are located in the southwestern edge of the Burren region of County Clare. The tallest of the cliffs stand at 702 feet, and it was near there that Karen was sketching when an attractive Irishman with a large sketchbook stood beside her.

They began talking about art and showing one another their work. He remarked that her detailed drawings and watercolors would sell well in his local gallery. He was a widower and encouraging and kind. To escape the wind, they strolled to the coffee shop that is literally built into the nearby hillside.

Inside she told him about her grandmother, who was born in the County Clare region. She mentioned her encounter with the old man in the faerie circle. How he somehow touched her. Healed her.

"I've heard stories about that old man," Karen's companion said. "He was an illustrator who lived in these parts long ago. He played an accordion, and some say he still looks after folks who pass by the faerie circles. But you must have met someone else, because the man I'm thinking of died a long time ago, in the nineteen hundreds. He's sort of a gentle ghost now."

Karen felt the hairs on her neck stand up slightly. "What was the old Irish gentleman's name?" she asked.

"Paddy," her companion said. "Paddy O'Flannigan."

CHAPTER 13

I MEET DEAD PEOPLE EVERY DAY

Air Canada flight 2019 touched down gently along the runway in Dublin, Ireland. We taxied to the gate and passengers jostled about, foraging and releasing stuffed overhead compartments. Through the plane's window, I spied the distant green hills of Ireland. Home to my long-deceased maternal grandparents. Finally, after a lifetime of excuses, I made it to Ireland.

I was traveling with my wife, eighteen-year-old son, brother-in-law, his wife, and their two young daughters. All of us are light packers, with only one carry-on bag and a small satchel apiece. Well, except for my brother-in-law's guitar, in its bulky protective case. He's part Irish and feels naked without his guitar close by.

Filing out of the airport in search of a Dublin taxi, we looked like ducks lined up in a row. Following one after another, with our rolling luggage cases in tow.

Travel, the necessary evil
A lot of people wax poetic about the wonders and joys of travel. Much of what they say is true. You'll experience new things and places and cultures. Your foreign trips will produce memories and

moments that will last a lifetime. It will fill you with creative ideas and inspire your artwork. But let's just be clear. Travel involves a lot of work and inconvenience.

One must plan out an itinerary, save the necessary funds, and set about packing intelligently. Absent a lot of travel experience, you just never pack exactly as you wish you had. Even for a minimalist packer like me. Something is always included that you don't need, and something you do need will be left behind.

Then there's the joys of airport security, with the lines and crying children and every manner of humanity nearly stripping to stand spread eagle on security scanners. There's paperwork and passports and foreign currency to comprehend. Overpriced airport food and plane bathrooms built for hobbits.

Let's not forget the annoying passenger next to you, who either talks your ear off or snores the whole flight. Usually, next to the screaming child.

Add to these indignities the fact that I get claustrophobic on planes and don't like heights. Yes, my doctor can prescribe "a little something" to take the edge off. Problem is, I never lose sight of the fact that I'm essentially sitting in a small sofa chair, hurtling across the sky at six hundred miles per hour and thirty-seven thousand feet high. Sounds almost dreamy, until the severe turbulence kicks in over Greenland.

Even the CNN news anchor Anderson Cooper, in his book *Dispatches from the Edge: A Memoir of War, Disasters and Survival*, acknowledged that some aspects of travel can be no fun. Yet he argues that the stressful moments and inconveniences are part of the whole experience. As every good story requires a bit of tension, so too every trip is made memorable by the ups and downs.

Travel is a necessary evil, because the payoff is worth all the trouble. Travel broadens our perspectives. Educates us about the world and how other people live. Travel reminds us how small we are. And most importantly, travel separates us from the dead people among us.

I meet dead people every day

Twenty-six years of police work have introduced me to a wide variety of people. From kind and heroic to cruel and sadistic. Interspersed among them are some of the saddest. I call them "the dead people."

We encounter them every day. People who are going through the motions in life but don't know why. People who gave up on their dreams or let life beat them down. They abandoned their bodies and physical health. People who perhaps felt the world owed them something. Or who just became bitter and negative.

There is no judgment here. Any one of us, at any time, could become sidetracked. A death in the family. A divorce. An illness. Such tragedies and challenges in life happen. Fortunately, with determination, professional help, and family/friend's support, we can rebound. But then some people remain mired in their own unhappiness. They wallow in it.

In Richard Paul Evans book, *The Walk*, a kind woman who works in a diner shared this nugget of wisdom:

> I meet dead people at the diner every day. People who have given up. That's all death requires of us, to give up living. The thing is, the only real sign of life is growth. And growth requires pain. So to choose life is to accept pain. Some people go to such lengths to avoid pain that they give up on life. They bury their hearts or they drink themselves numb until they don't feel anything anymore. The irony is, in the end their escape becomes more painful than what they are avoiding. Ultimately we decided whether our lives are good or bad, ugly or beautiful. Some people in this world have stopped looking for beauty, then

wonder why their lives are so ugly. Everyone carries divinity in them. Only through helping others can we save ourselves.

The luck of the Irish

When people joke about the "luck of the Irish," they often overlook how unlucky the Irish were. Whether facing foreign rulers or internal battles between Protestants and Catholics, the Irish have experienced their fair share of bad luck. But here's the amazing part. The Irish somehow retain this wonderful pluck and cheerful, upbeat attitude.

Visit any Irish pub and listen to the music. Watch as the old and young alike hoist pints of Guinness and sing their songs of country and loss and love. The Irish are a happy people, despite the struggles and hardships of life. They just choose to be.

I know what you're thinking. It's too hard to "just choose to be" happy. Certainly some days are better than others. I don't think a constant state of happiness is possible. Bad things come along as well as good things. However, one thing I saw consistently in Ireland was a charitable spirit. Young folks helping old folks. People holding doors open. Motorists rarely honking at one another. And there were pots of colorful flowers in just about every window I passed by.

There's a secret ingredient that will insulate you from becoming one of the living dead. That ingredient is a charitable heart. To develop a charitable heart, you have to stop thinking about yourself all the time. About seeking attention all the time. I think many of the Irish have figured this out, and that's why they're so cheerful.

Wisdom from a Benedictine monk

In author Tony Hendra's poignant book *Father Joe*, we meet a kindly, stuttering, Benedictine monk who maintains a lifelong friendship with Hendra, offering pearls of wisdom throughout.

Listen here as Father Joe offers Tony Hendra some sound advice: "Feelings are a great gift, but they're treacherous if that's all we live for. They drive us back into ourselves, you see. What I want. What I feel. What I need. A man and a woman pass beyond just feelings at some point, don't they? That's when they start to know true love. The love of another. The joy in another's existence. The wonderful ways that the other person is not like you, nor you like them. What you said about the p-p-prison of self you felt you were in-that was very exact. Love releases you from the p-p-prison, you see."

Father Joe goes on with this additional gem: "What you must ask yourself, Tony dear, is this: do you do the work you've chosen with joy and gratitude? Do you do it conscientiously? Do you do it for others first and yourself second?"

In Ireland I saw a lot of kindhearted people going about their work conscientiously, with joy and gratitude. Just about every one of our cab drivers was outgoing, cheerful, and talkative. The repair man in our hotel took the time to say hello and ask me how my trip was going. The bus drivers and train conductors were equally helpful and kind. It's like they all found the divinity in their work. Not in their station or wealth or fame. Simply joy in doing their work well and helping others along the way.

Not that the Irish are immune to the walking dead. I did see some sad souls and unhappy people. But on balance, the ratio of upbeat and charitable people was much greater.

How to raise the dead
At the moment I'm gutting it out again at thirty-six thousand feet, on my return flight home from two splendid weeks in Ireland. The people of Ireland reintroduced me to this notion of upbeat work and charity toward others. It's something I want to refine in my own work.

Having read Tony Hendra's *Father Joe* on the flight to Ireland, I now know that the best way to help the "dead people" I meet every day is to show them kindness and love. Sometimes the simplest acts of charity can create a positive spark in a wayward soul. A smile or door held open might help another to remember that "I do matter."

I also learned from *Father Joe* to focus more on doing my artwork with joy, gratitude, and conscientiousness. Remembering to not make it about me. Make it about others. Create art to bring joy to others.

So you see, all this from a two-week trip to Ireland. I still hate flying and all the attendant headaches of travel. But would I do it again? Absolutely. I hope you find the time to travel more yourself and nurture the kind of cheerfulness and peace our friends in Ireland demonstrate. The world would be a much happier place if we could all do that.

CHAPTER 14

NO, IT'S NOT TOO LATE

Maggie set her glass of chardonnay down, smiled at the group, and said, "I can't tell you how much I've enjoyed working with you all. It just doesn't seem real. I've been in this design firm for twenty-five years. I feel ancient!"

Everyone smiled and then Phillip, her boss, raised a glass. "A toast to Maggie Fuentes! Thank you for your expertise, loyalty, and friendship. May your well-earned retirement open new doors and happiness!" Applause erupted as the festive balloons bounced around them in the wine bar.

"Thanks, Phil. Thanks, everyone," Maggie said. She looked down at her wine glass for a moment. "I just wish Edward could have been here. We used to dream about this moment. About our next chapter."

Maggie's best friend Melissa gave her a hug, knowing how much Maggie missed Edward. Knowing that husbands are supposed to be there when you retire from a long career. To tell you how proud they are of you. To embrace you and take you home. Make you coffee the next morning and say, "So, what do you want to do today?"

Edward's pancreatic cancer took him too soon, and Maggie was retiring to an unknown future. Still, she put on a brave face, held up her retirement plaque, and said, "Thanks again, you guys!"

The invisible woman
Maggie had been unable to have children. She and Edward considered adoption when they were younger but eventually focused on their careers. Over the last few years, Maggie complained to Edward that she was becoming an old woman. Her hair had grayed; her eyes required glasses, and despite yoga and walking, it was harder to keep the weight down.

"You're a beautiful woman, inside and out," sweet Edward would always say. And while she owned a dynamite smile, big brown eyes, and attractive features, she knew that the passage of time can be unkind.

"I was walking into Starbucks yesterday," Maggie told Melissa a few weeks after her retirement, "and these three good-looking young men were strolling out. The three of them walked right past me. It was like I was invisible."

Melissa frowned and put her hand on Maggie's shoulder. "Sweetie, you're a beautiful, smart, talented woman."

Maggie smiled at the comment and said, "Yeah, but let's face it. When you're in your sixties, fewer men turn around and admire you. It's not that I want to reclaim my youth. I guess I just feel kinda adrift and alone."

Melissa gazed at a small painting on the wall of Maggie's living room. "Didn't you paint that?"

Both women gazed at the artwork, and Maggie said, "Yeah, I painted that five years ago. The design firm sent several of us to take a workshop with an amazing California artist named Kathleen Dunphy, to help us improve our landscape art. It was wonderful. We painted in the foothills of the Sierra Nevada. Edward and I talked about me getting into fine art, but I never did much with it."

Melissa smiled and said, "Maybe it's time you revisited that."

The wisdom of Christopher Reeves

The following week Maggie was getting her mail when she came across her neighbor, Douglas. Douglas was a paraplegic military veteran, confined to a wheelchair ever since an IED in Iraq altered the trajectory of his life. He was also an accomplished watercolor artist, and Maggie realized he might have some tips to help her dive into fine art.

"Douglas, may I invite you over for some coffee and scones? Now that I'm retired from the design firm, I'm thinking about getting back into fine art. I'd love to get your advice."

Douglas grinned and said, "You know, each scone requires about fifteen laps around the neighborhood to work off! But you have a date."

Later, at Maggie's house, she brought a tray with coffee and scones and the two talked. Maggie shared her feelings of uncertainty. "I feel lost, Douglas. Maybe it's too late to start over with a fine art career?"

"You know, Maggie, after Iraq I thought my life was over. But then I remembered how much I loved artwork. I used to enjoy watercolors and started back up. I fell in love with artists like Keiko Tenabe and Brienne Brown. So I took workshops, painted like crazy, and now I'm selling work in several galleries."

"That's amazing, Douglas. But I'm in my sixties. Even if I get back into painting, I feel like I'm too old to accomplish much with it." Maggie frowned as she said this.

"Maggie, do you know what the actor Christopher Reeves once said? 'I think a hero is an ordinary individual who finds strength to persevere and endure in spite of overwhelming obstacles.' I love that quote. Besides, there are lots of artists who found success later in life." With that, Douglas took a sip of coffee and nibbled on his scone.

"Oh really, name one," Maggie said.

"Millard Kaufman wrote his first novel, *Bowl of Cherries*, when he was ninety years old. Kathryn Bigelow was nearly sixty when she directed *The Hurt Locker* and *Zero Dark Thirty*. She won an Academy Award.

"The artist Louise Bourgeois created drawings, prints, and sculptures all her life but only became well known in her early seventies after a 1982 retrospective at the Museum of Modern Art in New York." Douglas took another bite of his scone, pleased with himself.

"Wow, I guess it's never too late to chase your passion and follow your dreams," Maggie said. "All this time, I've been feeling sorry for myself. I guess I should dust off my French easel and get busy painting?" She smiled at Douglas, admiring his spirit and wisdom. And then he leaned forward and said something very profound.

"Maggie, we celebrate beauty, youth, and child prodigies. We overlook the determined souls who overcome obstacles and whose stunning accomplishments arrive later in life. To achieve in one's golden years, despite the indignities of aging, is more remarkable to me than the early success of some wunderkind. It's not too late, Maggie. It's not too late to embrace the next chapter of your life!"

No, it's not too late
Inspired by Douglas's wisdom, Maggie found her old French easel in the attic and threw herself back into painting. Much to her surprise, she hadn't forgotten how to craft a pleasing painting. She remembered many of the lessons Kathleen Dunphy taught her.

With summer just a few weeks away, Maggie decided it was time to take a workshop and update her artistic skills. She always admired the artwork of Scott L. Christensen and decided to travel to Victor, Idaho, and attend one of his workshops. She knew the workshops were popular and filled up fast.

Maggie phoned Christensen's studio and spoke with an assistant about the upcoming workshop. "I'm recently retired and praying that there's still room in the workshop," Maggie pleaded.

The assistant was pleasant and kind, stating, "Let me check the roster and see."

Maggie thought of her late husband, Edward, and her friend Melissa's kind support. She remembered her workshop with Kathleen Dunphy in California. She reflected on her neighbor Douglas and his uplifting encouragement. She held her breath as the workshop assistant checked the roster. And then the assistant said, "No, it's not too late. We have one opening left."

A few tears of joy came to Maggie's eyes. "No, it's not too late," Maggie said to the assistant. "Not too late at all. Go ahead and sign me up."

CHAPTER 15

HOW YOUR HEART CAN IMPROVE YOUR ART

Put your ear down close to your soul and listen hard.

—Anne Sexton

This happened several years ago, but the memory of that day remains crystalline in my mind. It was a blessed Saturday and I was exhausted. I just got off night shift after a busy week at the police department. There had been many arrests, paperwork, and a difficult personnel matter to resolve. In short, I was spent and ready for a relaxing weekend.

I slept from 7:00 a.m. until 1:00 p.m. Groggy, I fixed a strong cup of coffee and started thinking about my Saturday afternoon. I was anxious to dive into my artwork. There's nothing better than a free day to immerse yourself in your passion.

Unbeknownst to me, my little boy had other plans. He ambled into my studio with his Buzz Lightyear action toy. "Dad, let's go watch *Toy Story*," he said sweetly, with earnest eyes and a smile. My wife had left to visit a friend for the afternoon, so it was just me and my son.

To infinity and beyond!
I abandoned my sketchbook and settled onto the couch. My son clicked on the DVD player, and soon we were watching the antics of Woody and Buzz Lightyear. Not long after, the doorbell rang, and we were surprised by the unexpected visit of a friend from Oregon.

It quickly became apparent that my free afternoon of artwork and relaxation wasn't going to happen. My friend from Oregon was an amateur survivalist and had come to town to take a tracking and wilderness survival course. He started to tell my son all about it and soon they were itching to go hiking.

Since we live on the central coast of California, our backyard is literally the Santa Cruz Mountains, with redwoods and miles of mountain trails. It was a beautiful, sunny day. We gathered some water and snacks and headed outdoors.

Throughout our hike my friend pointed out different animal tracks to my son and explained which berries were edible. As much as I wanted to spend the afternoon doing artwork, I had to admit I was enjoying myself. At one point we came to a clearing and discovered a huge tree stump. My son and I climbed on top, and we yelled, "To infinity and beyond!" My friend snapped a quick photo of the special moment.

The days are long, but the years are short
I remember once reading an article on parenting. It included this poignant observation about raising children: "The days are long, but the years are short."

That Saturday afternoon in the woods with my son turned out to be a wonderful experience and splendid memory. We ended up having dinner with my friend and enjoyed some laughs about our adventure.

Had I been selfish and turned down this opportunity, I know I would have hated myself and been unable to enjoy my artwork. Sometimes you just have to give into the moment and go with it.

After dinner my friend left, and I took my worn-out little boy home. A warm bath, pajamas, and soon he slipped off into slumberland. I tucked him in and ambled into my studio. Amazingly, the day had invigorated me and my creativity flowed. The resulting artwork pleased me.

The superpower in us all
My father once witnessed an elderly man get struck by a car in town. The man was thrown quite a distance and badly injured. My dad rendered aid and learned that the man was a homeless, Italian immigrant who lived in a small cabin he built in the woods. The old man's name was Ted Strollo.

My father was an administrative-law judge. He commuted via train Monday through Friday to San Francisco to work. It was over an hour commute to and from work. Most nights Dad came home after 6:00 p.m. Weekends were the only time he had to relax and recharge. Nevertheless, Dad didn't hesitate to help "Mr. Strollo."

Dad followed the ambulance to the hospital, gave a statement to the police, and ended up providing legal assistance to Mr. Strollo. Dad was able to get him financial assistance and secured him an apartment in town.

For several years after that, Dad took time out of his weekends to visit Mr. Strollo. Dad always brought him gifts during the holidays, too. Through my father I learned that there is a superpower in us all, if we choose to use it. That superpower is charity and kindness.

I remember asking Dad why he sacrificed so much of his weekend time to visit Mr. Strollo. Dad replied, "He doesn't have anyone else, Johnny. I'd feel bad all week if I didn't pay him a visit."

I suppose Dad was channeling the wisdom of Plato: "Be kind, for everyone you meet is fighting a harder battle."

Give and you shall receive
Many are familiar with the biblical passage in Luke 6:38: "Give, and it will be given to you." When we listen to our hearts and help others, it invariably comes back on us in positive ways. We improve our self-esteem, which fosters better health and happiness.

I created better art after my day in the woods with my son. My father would have been conflicted and less focused at work had he not helped Mr. Strollo. Heck, things even turned out great for Buzz Lightyear because he stood up for his friends in *Toy Story*!

Your heart can help your art. When we listen to our hearts, we do the right thing and help others. Doing so uplifts our spirit, which invariably opens the floodgates of creativity.

I'll close with this bit of wisdom from Canadian writer Charles de Lint: "I don't want to live in the kind of world where we don't look out for each other. Not just the people who are close to us, but anybody who needs a helping hand. I can't change the way anybody else thinks, or what they choose to do, but I can do my bit."

CHAPTER 16

HOW TO AVOID THE RENAISSANCE-MAN TRAP

When I was a boy, my mother enrolled me in classical piano lessons. Every Friday after school I was dropped off at the home of my piano teacher, Irma Hincenbergs. Mrs. Hincenbergs was a Latvian refugee who lived in a beautiful Victorian house in downtown Los Gatos, California.

On the wall beside Mrs. Hincenbergs's grand piano were several pencil drawings of famous composers, such as Chopin and Beethoven. I often admired the drawings as I butchered my way through Debussy's "Clair de Lune."

Mrs. Hincenbergs knew that I loved to draw cartoons. Every Friday after my lesson, she presented me with a stack of editorial cartoons cut out of her daily newspapers. She was such a kind and thoughtful woman.

Despite all my grumbling about lost Friday afternoons, I grew to appreciate classical piano. It created the foundation for my later experiences playing keyboards and singing in both high school and college rock bands.

I didn't realize at the time how much my interactions with Mrs. Hincenbergs were shaping my creative predilections for music, drawing, and cartooning. Further, I had no inkling of how much these diverse interests would complicate my life.

The Leonardo da Vinci curse

Leonardo da Vinci was clearly a remarkable polymath. Painter, sculptor, anatomist, architect. Talk about a multitalented individual! He was definitely born in the right era, as the Renaissance rewarded men of such varied talents and dimensions. But would Leonardo have fared so well today?

According to author Leonardo Lospennato, who wrote *The Da Vinci Curse—Life Design for People with Too Many Interests and Talents*, Leonardo da Vinci might have struggled in our modern age. Why? Because our knowledge base has increased exponentially from the days of the Renaissance.

In this age of vast information, a multifaceted guy like Leonardo da Vinci would've had a field day indulging his many interests. However, he may have struggled to make a good living due to all his intellectual curiosities.

Increasingly, we rely on specialists rather than generalists. For example, you wouldn't use a general practitioner for open heart surgery. You'd seek out a cardiac surgeon. Similarly, most college students today declare a major in order to have a solid career path.

Depth versus knowledge

As a teenager I juggled many creative pursuits. I played the piano and sang. I liked to paint and draw. I became a cartoonist for my high school newspaper. I enjoyed writing short stories. Beyond these creative hobbies, I also played chess and competitive tennis and studied the martial arts.

I became what the author Leonardo Lospennato calls a "Da Vinci person." Da Vinci people dabble in many areas. They tend to jump around from field to field, acquiring a lot of knowledge but not necessarily a lot of depth. Jacks of all trades but masters of none.

Friends often referred to me as the "Renaissance man" because of all my creative pursuits. The problem was I wasn't progressing very fast in any of my interests. I was spread too thin and had fallen into the Renaissance-man trap.

The book "*The Da Vinci Curse*" recommends finding a single pursuit that is "complex" enough to integrate many of your talents. One way to figure this out is by using a preselection strategy. Examine your creative interests and look for three criteria:

1. Is it fun?
2. Do you have a talent for it?
3. Can you earn money doing it?

A lot of artists and creative people dabble in many areas but never achieve mastery in any one pursuit. They become frustrated because they aren't getting anywhere. This was my story for a long time. Only when I gave up all the hobbies and focused exclusively on my art did I see progress.

The power of simplifying
Simplicity played a big part in helping me avoid the Renaissance-man trap. Early in my law-enforcement career, I was dabbling in many hobbies, from music and martial arts to writing and cartooning. With a family and full-time job, I often grew frustrated trying to squeeze my hobbies into very little free time.

I asked myself which hobbies I enjoyed the most and had talent for. The answer then was clearly my cartooning. I was a decent martial artist and musician, but my cartooning was already at a professional level.

So, I quit training in jujitsu (despite being a brown belt on the cusp of my black belt). I knew I could always play and sing the piano at home, but I gave up on putting together a new band.

Guess what happened? My cartooning blossomed. I ended up moonlighting as a staff editorial cartoonist for both my city and county newspapers. I began selling my work and found deeper creative satisfaction. All because I simplified and set aside the other hobbies.

Routines trump goals
Focusing on one area of expertise will enable you to acquire greater depth and ability. It will keep you out of the Renaissance-man trap. However, this doesn't mean you should abandon your intellectual curiosity.

The website lifehacker.com ran an article that somewhat contradicts what I have written here. The article is titled "Knowing a Little of Everything Is Often Better than Having One Expert Skill." The article notes:

> Creativity often requires drawing analogies between one body of knowledge and another. Pablo Picasso merged Western art techniques with elements of African art. He was struck by the way African artists combined multiple perspectives into a single work, and that helped lead to the development of cubism. Similarly, great scientists often draw parallels between different areas to create new ideas. In the history of science, Johannes Kepler struggled to understand how the planets could move around the sun, and drew on his knowledge of light and magnetism to try to understand the force that moved the planets.

There's no doubt that reading widely and acquiring diverse knowledge can broaden your perspectives, enrich your life, and quite possibly improve your art. But if every pursuit of yours is given equal time, then you run the risk of falling into the Renaissance-man trap.

Blogger James Clear has written about how routines trump goals. You may have the goal of becoming a top artist, but it's the routines and habits you adopt that will ultimately matter most. To that end, set up a regular schedule and focus on deep work in the passion you love most. Put as much time into that as you can, and in this way you'll avoid the Renaissance-man trap and succeed more quickly.

CHAPTER 17

THIS IS HOW OLD TREES SPEAK TO US

We met unceremoniously. I stepped into a clearing and there she was. Bespectacled and stooped over her dilapidated French easel. She eyed me warily but soon turned her attention back to the canvas. Despite her gray hair and advanced years, she scooted back and forth gingerly.

"I have to step away from the piece to see the whole. That's how I find the false junctures." Her voice startled me.

"The false junctures?" I asked, confused.

"Yes, the false junctures. The places where things don't connect properly." She squinted at me, assessing. Then she put down her brushes and reached into a backpack on the ground. "Care for a drink?" she offered. Much to my surprise, she pulled out a flask.

"Uh, no, thanks, I don't drink. I have no talent for it." It was the truth. My father was an alcoholic, and I inherited the same proclivity. Sins of the father, sins of the son. I lacked an on/off switch, so I steer clear of drinking.

"I admire that," she said just before taking a swig. "What's the line in that Clint Eastwood movie?" she asked. "Oh yes, 'A man's got to know his limitations.' I love Dirty Harry. He says it like it is." She belched and took another sip.

I'm pretty sure my mouth was agape with incredulity. I'd been hiking these trails for the last three years in order to get away from people and be alone. To think and try to figure out the mess of my life. I miss my six-year-old daughter. Divorce and visitation every other weekend were all my ex and the courts allowed.

"Hey, where'd you go just now?" the old woman asked.

"Oh, sorry. I'm not used to running into people out here." I gave her a half smile.

"People can be a distraction when you're running away from life." She set down the flask and plopped beside her backpack. "Young man, I'm a widowed and retired old woman. But if you like, I'll share with you a few things." As she spoke the wind danced through the tree leaves. Everything felt so surreal.

"Okay, why not," I said as I sat down with this enigmatic old woman in the woods.

Life is a lot like parking lots
She told me that she used to teach literature in the English department at the local university. Her husband Alfred passed away nine years ago, and she lived alone now. Her only daughter had grown up. Just a Siamese cat, her books and love of outdoor painting.

I told her I was a sales rep for an athletic clothing company. Been through a nasty divorce and only saw my daughter every other weekend. I told her my drinking was partly why I was divorced. Been sober a few years now. I admitted that I just don't care much for other people. "I thought I'd be much further along by now with my life," I admitted.

The old woman smiled and said, "I heard this Israeli writer on NPR recently. He said something like, 'We all think we are the star, the one whose name is on the marque, and everyone else are bit players. But everyone else thinks they are the star. Just like parking lots, we are all looking for our space.'"

She gazed at me a moment and asked, "Do you enjoy your work?"

I thought about that and said, "Yeah, I do. It's challenging but fulfilling. But for some reason, I still feel kind of empty. Lonely, maybe. I guess I'm not a happy-go-lucky type."

She took another swig from her flask and said, "Friedrich Nietzsche said, 'There is one thing one has to have: either a soul that is cheerful by nature, or a soul that is cheerful by work, love, art and knowledge.' Sounds like your work is fine, but the love, art, and knowledge need work."

The hidden life of trees
We sat together silently for a moment, watching the trees as they swayed in the wind. Then she spoke. "You know, I just finished a fascinating book, titled *The Hidden Life of Trees*. The forest is a social network. Trees actually communicate and support one another. They can sense with their leaves and roots and fit into one another's respective ecosystems. Without trees to draw water inland, we'd all be in trouble."

I gazed at her, mesmerized. This elderly sage in the woods. I closed my eyes and listened as she continued, "When Scots pine trees are attacked by caterpillars, they release a scent from pheromones in their leaves. This pheromone attracts wasps who come and lay eggs in the leaves, which turn into larvae that eat the caterpillars. Some trees send out electric signals via fungal fibers underground that spread out for several miles, informing other trees of conditions. It's sort of like 'tree e-mail.' People don't appreciate how much trees communicate and support one another."

It was fascinating but I had to ask, "Why are you sharing this with me?"

She got quiet for a moment. Then she said, "See all those leaves shimmering in the light and dancing in the breeze around us. Can you feel the peace in that? This is how old trees speak to us."

"And what are they saying?" I asked, somewhat amused but curious.

"They're trying to tell us that we are just like them. Both isolated and connected. We must lay down roots and establish our presence. But we must build alliances and connections, too. Trees take the long view, just as we should plan for our future. Trees don't blame. They take responsibility for themselves."

"You're making trees sound a tad anthropomorphic, aren't you?" I pointed out.

"No, I'm saying we can learn a lot from trees. Maybe I'm analogizing a bit, but think about it. Trees are admirably independent. Strong yet connected to others. Meanwhile, we're such fragile creatures. Always worrying about what others think. As Lao Tzu noted, 'Care what other people think, and you will always be their prisoner.' We need to get comfortable with our individuality, like trees, yet leverage the power of community, too. Nobody should be lonely in life."

A good life is like a good painting
I asked the old woman her name and she said, "Carole Ann." I told her that I went on hikes to figure out my unhappiness. My work was fulfilling; I was healthy and enjoyed my hobbies of hiking and camping. But something was missing.

"Remember when you first bumped into me?" she said. "I was talking about finding the 'false junctures' in a painting? The places where things don't connect properly? Well, that's what you need to figure out in your life. You see, a good life is like a good painting. You have to smooth out some of those rough edges and be sure to have proper values. And to balance out the grayness, you need a little color, too."

The sun was setting, and it was starting to get chilly. I thanked Carole for all her wisdom and advice. From trees to art, my head was swirling with everything she told me. I hiked back to my jeep and made my way to town, deciding to pick up a hot latte at the local Starbucks.

As I sat down to sip my latte, a pretty woman sat across from me. She said I looked familiar and I told her where I worked. Turns out she just began working in the local Patagonia store, and she remembered me from a sales meeting. Recently divorced, she moved to town for a fresh start and to be closer to her mother.

"What does your mother do?" I asked.

She smiled and said, "Oh, she's a retired literature professor. But now she just drives me crazy talking about trees and painting."

"Carole Ann?" I said.

"Why yes, do you know her?" the woman asked.

"Yes, she helped me understand what the false juncture was in my life."

"The 'false juncture'?" she asked.

"Yeah, it's the place where things don't connect properly."

"Did my mom tell you about one of the largest living organisms on earth? It's a grove of quaking aspen trees in Utah called the Pando. It's a forest, but all of its forty-seven thousand aspen trees come from a single root system spread over one hundred and six acres in Utah." She smiled at me.

I offered to get her another coffee and she accepted. Maybe old trees really do speak to us. Like the Pando in Utah, maybe people are all connected, too. How else to explain meeting Carole Ann in the woods and now her daughter?

All I knew was that the "false juncture" in my life seemed to disappear. Things were beginning to connect again. And a feeling dormant for so long was resurfacing. The feeling we all long for. The feeling we all deserve in our lives. Maybe old trees feel it too. It's called happiness.

CHAPTER 18
THIS MUCH I KNOW IS TRUE

Carol dropped Timothy off at the day care and headed to work. Being a dental hygienist was not her idea of a lifelong career, but it paid the bills and ensured independence for her and Timothy.

At five years old, Timothy was too young to understand divorce. All he knew was that Daddy visited every other weekend and Mommy was his rock. Whenever nightmares came, Mommy was there to soothe him back to sleep. When he was hungry, Mommy had a special way of making pancakes or chicken nuggets. His favorite comfort food.

Carol dated periodically, but her true passion was painting. She studied landscape painting at community college and managed to take a few workshops.

The rhythms of work and parenting consumed most of her time, but there were golden windows of creativity. Holidays and weekends off, when Timothy was in day care and she could immerse herself in her art.

Be a good steward of your gifts
Many evenings, when Timothy was asleep and the pace of life slowed, Carol would brew a cup of soothing tea and settle into

some reading. Her favorite poet was Jane Kenyon and her collection of essays, "*A Hundred White Daffodils.*"

Jane Kenyon was a poet and American translator. Her work was simple, spare, and emotionally resonant. She penned poems of rural images, haylofts bathed in sun light and shorn winter fields. She wrestled with bouts of depression and "having it out with melancholy." For some reason, Carol identified with Jane Kenyon. Kenyon had her struggles, just like Carol, but somehow she conjured beauty through her poetry.

Carol's favorite Jane Kenyon line was this: "Be a good steward of your gifts. Protect your time. Feed your inner life. Avoid too much noise. Read good books, have good sentences in your ears. Be by yourself as often as you can. Walk. Take the phone of the hook. Work regular hours."

Carol knew that Kenyon's advice was primarily for writers, but it held value for painters as well. Yes, Carol had a day job as a dental hygienist as well as her responsibilities as a mother. But there were slivers of time that demanded Carol's attention. Slivers of time to hone her craft as a representational painter. She needed to be a "good steward" of her gifts.

There's only now
Carol loved good music and serendipitously discovered the recordings of actor and musician Hugh Laurie. She enjoyed listening to his piano compositions and found inspiration in his music as she painted.

Once she researched Hugh Laurie and found this quote of his: "It's a terrible thing, I think, in life to wait until you're ready. I have this feeling now that actually no one is ever ready to do anything. There's almost no such thing as ready. There's only now. And you may as well do it now. I mean, I say that confidently as if I'm about to go bungee jumping or something—I'm not. I'm not a crazed risk taker. But I do think that, generally speaking, now is as good a time as any."

Hugh Laurie inspired Carol to put up a website of her paintings. It was scary and exhilarating and fun. She photographed her best work and signed up with a wonderful online art website service to promote her art. But when she uploaded her work to the world, the response was largely crickets. She loved painting, but clearly her work needed refinement.

Time passed and despite her best efforts, Carol's work sold irregularly. She dreamed of becoming a successful artist and leaving her day job as a dental hygienist. But try as she might to vary her artistic approach, she seemed incapable of growing her collector base. So she focused on raising Timothy and painted along the margins of her schedule.

Mending the broken
Wikipedia describes the origins of Goodwill Industries as follows: "In 1902, Reverend Edgar J. Helms of Morgan Methodist Chapel in Boston, started Goodwill as part of his ministry. Helms and his congregation collected used household goods and clothing being discarded in wealthier areas of the city, then trained and hired the unemployed or bereft to mend and repair them. The products were then redistributed to those in need or were given to the needy people who helped repair them."

Carol liked the mission and work of the Goodwill and often shopped there because so many of their products were affordable. And so much of the Goodwill's mission focused on mending the broken souls in society.

One weekend, when Timothy was on a playdate, Carol spent some time at the local Goodwill store, exploring deals and products. She came upon a lovely little tonal painting of a quiet mountain scene. The work was more restrained than her own landscapes. Simple, subdued, and yet bursting with vitality and character.

On a whim, she decided to buy the piece and hang it in her apartment studio. The elegant signature "Delgado" was unfamiliar to her, but she liked the piece nonetheless.

Light at the end of the tunnel
The years passed, and Carol quietly raised Timothy into a fine young man. He had an affinity for computer science and after college secured a promising position as an engineer with Google.

Timothy found a lovely condo, and his career was progressing nicely. Carol couldn't help but feel a sense of pride and accomplishment. Her years as a dental hygienist made it possible to pay for Timothy's education. Timothy's father contributed little, which only added to Carol's sense of accomplishment in raising him.

One day Timothy phoned Carol and confided that he had struggled somewhat the past year at work. Fortunately, despite a few difficult quarters, he had prevailed and done well professionally. In fact, he was on the cusp of a significant promotion.

He mentioned a small painting of hers that hung in his apartment. "Mom, every time I doubted myself, I looked at your painting. The one of the haystacks in sunlight. I don't know why, but every time I looked at it, I felt a sense of hope. Kinda like a light at the end of the tunnel. And you know what, it helped me get through this year. It's what led to my promotion."

His words meant so much to her. The idea that her artwork inspired him to succeed. Perhaps she had not attained fame and fortune with her art. But at least it helped her son find greater success. At least it was his "light at the end of the tunnel." Still, she was frustrated by the sense that she failed as an artist. That her lack of commercial success meant her art was insignificant and pedestrian.

The true measure of a life
Carol's cat Winston was an inquisitive soul. Unfortunately, his curious nature often led to mishaps. So it was one Saturday evening when Winston was pawing the small painting above the bookcase.

Carol heard a crash and ran into the living room. Winston stared at her, frozen atop the bookcase. There on the floor was the small tonal painting by Delgado. The one she plucked from obscurity at the Goodwill. As she picked it up, she noticed that the back side paper was torn. And much to her surprise, within the paper was a small envelope.

Carol slipped out the envelope and opened it, finding a letter within. She unfolded the letter, revealing a beautiful copperplate cursive. Carrying the letter into the lamp light, she read. And this is what the letter said:

> To the person holding this letter, thank you for purchasing my painting. I am an old man and there is little of life left in me. Artwork and painting have been my passion. I've had to perform other jobs and work to support my family, but painting has been everything to me. As Saul Bellow said, "I feel that art has something to do with the achievement of stillness in the midst of chaos. A stillness which characterizes prayer, too, and the eye of the storm. I think that art has something to do with an arrest of attention in the midst of distraction."
>
> Artwork and creative expression are gifts we give ourselves, the ones we love and others. We might dream of artistic fame and recognition, but this is not the purpose of art. The purpose of art is to touch others. To inspire, move, instigate thought and remind all that the true measure of a life is love, authenticity and meaningful contribution.
>
> Do not burden yourself with regrets, unfulfilled dreams and sadness. If you have loved truly; if you have improved the lives of others; if you have raised well-adjusted children; then you have lived a worthwhile life. Your artistic expression, whether widely recognized or obscure, reflects your deepest humanity and spirit. And that is enough.
>
> —Alphonse Delgado

This much I know is true
The world is awash in opinions. Online gurus and self-help authors dispense formulas and directives on how others should live. The problem is that no two people are exactly alike. What might work for some may not work for others. Carol understood this, and yet Alphonse Delgado's heartfelt wisdom struck a deep chord in her.

Carol held the letter in her hands, her eyes misty with a sort of emotional resonance, when she was startled by the phone ringing. She answered, "Hello?"

"Hi, Mom," said Timothy, "You know that girl at work I told you about? Nicole? Well, you won't believe this. She's an artist. An oil painter just like you. We've been dating for six months now. She could be the one."

"That's wonderful, honey," Carol said.

"Mom, she was looking at your painting last night. The one of the haystacks. She said it reminds her of her grandfather's art. He was a real-estate broker by day and painter by night. She told me he used to say, 'So much of life is uncertain and hard. But this much I know is true: Art is the best of us. Art reveals our souls. Our deepest truths. It need not fetch fame or fortune to be true and authentic.' Isn't that wonderful, Mom?"

"Why yes, son, that's beautiful. Nicole's grandfather sounds like a wise man. What is his name?"

"Delgado. Alphonse Delgado," Timothy said, unaware of the magical joy filling his mother's heart.

CHAPTER 19

THIS IS HOW ABANDONING THE HERD CAN BRING SUCCESS

We live in a society where most people will take the escalator rather than the stairs. Because it's easier. Watch the patterns of movement in an airport or shopping mall. The hordes of people pour into elevators and escalators. Only a handful take the stairs.

Best-selling author and motivational speaker Rory Vaden wrote an excellent book, titled *"Take the Stairs: 7 Steps to Achieving True Success."* The book tells us that we should be more like buffalo than cows. Rory Vaden grew up in the state of Colorado, with its world famous Rocky Mountains. Colorado is evenly divided between the east and west, with the east containing the great Kansas plains. It's one of the few places in the world where cows and buffalo roam together.

When storms brew out of western Colorado, cows turn east to outrun them. The only problem is that cows are notoriously slow. They plod along in vain, trying to outrun the clouds and rain. Unfortunately, the storm soon overtakes them, and they are soaked beneath the pelting sheets of rain.

As Rory Vaden explains, "What buffalo do on the other hand is very unique for the animal kingdom. Buffalo wait for the storm to cross right over the crest of the peak of the mountaintop and as the storm rolls over the ridge the buffalo turn and charge directly into the storm."

Rory Vaden adds, "Instead of running east away from the storm they run west directly at the storm. By running at the storm they run straight through it. Minimizing the amount of pain and time and frustration they experience from that storm."

In other words, buffalo face their problems head-on. They don't run from them, procrastinate, or make excuses. Unlike most herds, buffalo dive into their problem and deal with it. Much like ripping the Band-Aid off, they "get it done."

The quest for the Inner Ring

C. S. Lewis was a British novelist, academic, and lay theologian who taught at Oxford University (Magdalen College) from 1925 to 1954. The website rzim.org examined C. S. Lewis's famous speech at Magdalen College, noting:

> During his tenure as a professor at Magdalen College in Oxford, C.S. Lewis delivered a memorial oration to the students of King's College, the University of London. It was titled "The Inner Ring." Addressing his young audience as "the middle-aged moralist," Lewis warned of the natural desire to find ourselves a part of the right inner circles, which exist endlessly and tauntingly throughout life. He cautioned about the consuming ambition to be an insider and not an outsider, on the right side of the right camp, though the lines that distinguish the camps are invisible, and the circle is never as perfect from within as it looks from without. Like the taunting mirage a weary traveler chases through the

desert, noted Lewis, the quest for the Inner Ring will break your heart unless you break it.

What C. S. Lewis was talking about is our superficial need to be a part of the "in crowd." More specifically, the "innermost circle." Such circles may or may not be at the top of an organization. They may be a secret, inner ring who control the actual goings-on of an organization or group.

For example, perhaps you join a particular art group. You know that penetrating the leadership or "inner circle" of such a group implies great things. Maybe you'll be able to add some impressive initials to the signature of your paintings. Or you'll be recognized as "important" and part of the "in crowd."

While it's true that knowing the "right people" can open doors, C. S. Lewis cautioned us about pursuing these inner rings. Sooner or later, once you're in, they lose their luster. Before long, you'll be searching for yet another ring.

Better to be the sound craftsmen
C. S. Lewis urged us to embrace our craft and forge our own path. Create our own "inner ring."

Here's how C. S. Lewis put it: "The quest of the Inner Ring will break your hearts unless you break it. But if you break it, a surprising result will follow. If in your working hours you make the work your end, you will presently find yourself all unawares inside the only circle in your profession that really matters. You will be one of the sound craftsmen, and other sound craftsmen will know it."

In other words, the cream rises to the top. Exceptional craftsmanship and exemplary art stands on its own. It doesn't require membership, alliances, or admission. Everyone recognizes it for what it is: great artwork.

As C. S. Lewis concluded: "And if in your spare time you consort simply with the people you like, you will again find that you have come unawares to a real inside: that you are indeed snug and safe at the centre of something which, seen from without, would look exactly like an Inner Ring. But the difference is that the secrecy is accidental, and its exclusiveness a by-product, and no one was led thither by the lure of the esoteric: for it is only four or five people who like one another meeting to do things that they like. This is friendship. Aristotle placed it among the virtues. It causes perhaps half of all the happiness in the world, and no Inner Ring can ever have it."

The subtle art of not caring
Mark Manson is a successful blogger and somewhat contrarian spirit. Despite his self-described "potty mouth" style of writing, his insights and conclusions about better living are fresh and often counterintuitive.

Manson's new book bucks most self-help platitudes about pursuing happiness. In fact, Manson argues that pursuing positivity actually leads to unhappiness. We want to feel good about ourselves, so we try to get in with the right crowd. We compare ourselves to others, seek shortcuts, and avoid negativity and pain at all costs.

Ironically, it's the negative experiences and difficult things that shape and help us grow more. Mark Manson argues that when we stop caring about what everyone else thinks and get comfortable with doing hard things, we'll grow more and be happier. For example, going to the gym and working out can be somewhat negative. It's hard work and not always fun. But by embracing the difficulty of it, we get in shape and feel better about ourselves.

The actor and martial artist Chuck Norris wrote an amazing foreword in the book "*Do Hard Things*," by the brothers Alex and Brett Harris. Chuck Norris noted:

> Today we live in a culture that promotes comfort, not challenges. Everything is about finding ways to escape hardship, avoid pain, and dodge duty.

Author Mark Manson argues that if someone is better than you at something, he or she probably "failed at it longer." Everyone wants success and recognition, but few are willing to embrace the pain to achieve it. Exceptional people are obsessive about improvement. They don't care what everyone else thinks. They just hunker down and do the hard work. They're buffalos, not cows.

Abandon the herd to succeed
The world of art is a competitive and difficult environment. Open any art magazine, and you'll encounter a lot of similar landscape, cityscape, still life, and figurative work. A lot of plein air art and atelier-trained figurative paintings are similar. Many are quite accomplished, but much of the work is duplicative.

Newer artists ape their instructors, and collectors look deeper for truly original, fresh work. It's not that being "different" alone will carry the day. Quality matters too.

The challenge for artists and creatives is to abandon the herd. Don't be like those cows, plodding along and getting soaked in the rain. Strive to be more like the buffalo and face the storm head-on. Dive in and do the hard work while everyone else is producing familiar but less original work. Push yourself further, embrace the struggle, and find that deeper, unique work inside yourself.

Adopt C. S. Lewis's argument and create your own "inner ring." Your own unique voice and style. When you do, others will be attracted to your work. They'll want to emulate it, and collectors will want to own it. You in turn will find greater fulfillment than merely copying what everyone else is doing.

By abandoning the herd and following Chuck Norris's advice to face your challenges, you'll forge your own artistic path. Take the stairs instead of the escalator. Charge head-on into the storm. Do hard things. Create your own "inner ring." In these ways you'll likely reach new heights with your creative work as well as a deeper sense of joy and fulfillment.

CHAPTER 20

THE FLOWER THIEF

Sergeant Peter Jensen had been with the Rockport Police Department for sixteen years, but he'd never seen a case like this. For the last two weeks, the calls came in from all over town. Always the same thing. An angry homeowner or gardener. Insistent that the police get to the bottom of it. After all, the spree of thefts had merited several newspaper articles. The theft of flowers, to these victims, was a serious crime!

There was Mr. Jacobs and his dahlias. He was a fastidious gardener. He didn't know who snipped off so many of his prized possessions, but he wanted blood. And, of course, Mrs. Idleberg, whose beautiful roses vanished in the middle of the day. "You must investigate this," she said in her Latvian accent, "because those roses...they were my babies."

Sergeant Jensen couldn't believe his luck. Of all the crazy cases to get stuck with. Really? Flower thefts? The other cops on his shift did what cops do. Teased him relentlessly. Sergeant Jensen found flowers in his locker. In his desk. One day he even found some rose petals in his uniform pockets!

Don't send me flowers when I'm dead

Walter Higgins's long career as an English butler prepared him well for Essex House, the Rockport bed and breakfast that he and his wife Mary bought eight years ago.

Walter's mother had passed away and left him a sizable inheritance, which he used to leave Britain and begin a new life as owner and operator of Essex House. Mary was an excellent chef, and Essex House became known as one of the finest B&Bs in town.

Having been a professional butler, Walter was a stickler for details. Beyond the immaculate rooms, hallways, linens, and fine dinner wines, Walter knew the power of a little color. Which is why he hired a top gardener to encircle Essex House with magnificent flower beds.

Walter's eye for details is what led to a break in Sgt. Jensen's case. "Last night around six, there was an elderly bloke with a backpack outside," Walter told Sgt. Jensen. "I went outside and asked him if he needed any help. The man looked at me and said, 'Don't send me flowers when I'm dead. If you like me, send them while I'm alive.' And then he walked off."

"Okay," said Sgt. Jensen. "Anything else?"

"I recognized the line he quoted. It's from Brian Clough. An English football player and manager. And one more thing. When he walked away, I saw one of our roses dangling from his backpack." Walter's eyes twinkled, clearly pleased with himself. "Do you think this is your flower thief?" Walter asked.

"Let's get our composite sketch guy to come over here and work on a drawing from your description. He's self-taught but pretty good. Once done, we'll post it around town. And thanks for all your help," Sgt. Jensen said.

The free soul is rare

Maria Contreras liked working at the Oceanview Residential Community. She had a soft spot for the elderly and a reverence for the grace and dignity of the greatest generation.

One resident in particular had broken Maria's heart. Esther Steinberg. She had been an art teacher who specialized in working with developmentally delayed children.

Esther could have been a notable artist, but she relinquished that path to help disabled children. "How sad," Maria often thought, "that Esther became disabled herself. All because of one crippling stroke."

One evening shift Maria saw the Rockport Police Department's "wanted man" flyer in the break room. She immediately recognized the face in the composite sketch. It was Morrie Steinberg, Esther's husband. He was a retired English professor.

Morrie was a fixture at Oceanview Residential Community. He visited Esther every day and placed fresh flowers all around her room. Even though Esther could no longer talk, the tears of joy in her eyes said everything. Morrie would hold her hand and often tell her that since she could no longer paint, he would paint her room for her. With colorful flowers.

Morrie once told Maria that his wife Esther was unique. "Few of us ever attain what Esther has. Through her art and working with children, she found a life of peace and grace. Like Charles Bukowski once wrote, 'The free soul is rare, but you know it when you see it—basically because you feel good, very good, when you are near or with them.' And that's how I've always felt with my Esther. So very good."

End of the journey

Maybe Maria suspected all along that Morrie was the flower thief. After all, the thefts had been in the papers for a few weeks now. And who could miss the abundance of fresh flowers all around Esther's room. But Maria knew that Morrie was on a fixed income and used most of his pension to pay for Esther's care.

With tears in her eyes, Maria finally made the call. It was the right thing to do. Sergeant Jensen arrived within the hour, and Maria told him everything about Morrie, Esther, and the daily flowers he brought.

That afternoon Sgt. Jensen sat in the lobby and waited for Morrie to arrive. Sure enough, Morrie strolled in with a large backpack on his shoulder.

Sergeant Jensen immediately recognized Morrie's likeness from the composite sketch. Morrie gazed over at Sgt. Jensen. He stopped walking and looked down toward Esther's room. Then back at Sgt. Jensen. "I suppose you're here for me," Morrie said.

For the next hour, Sgt. Jensen interviewed Morrie and got a full confession. "I used to buy her flowers. They made her so happy," Morrie explained. "But money got tight, so I 'liberated' some local color to make a disabled woman happy."

Sergeant Jensen couldn't help but think of his own wife, Jennifer. How they'd been struggling lately with the mortgage and in their relationship. Maybe if he adopted the same sacrifice and love for Jennifer as Morrie had for Esther, life would be better?

Sergeant Jensen said he admired Morrie. Stealing was wrong, but his heart was in the right place.

Morrie was quiet for a moment and then said, "Esther always said that we don't live in a coincidental universe. Things happen for a reason. As the author Wally Lamb wrote, 'The seeker embarks on a journey to find what he wants and discovers, along the way, what he needs.' Maybe we were meant to meet? Either way, I take full responsibility for my actions. Will you at least let me say good-bye to Esther before you take me in?"

There is a nobility in compassion
In the days that followed Morrie's arrest, the town was abuzz with gossip and letters to the editor. Some were unsympathetic and congratulated the Rockport Police Department for solving the case. Others felt sorry for Morrie but acknowledged that he shouldn't have stolen all those flowers. And then the following letter to the editor was printed in the *Rockport Herald*:

Dear Editor,

I'm a grade school English teacher. I couldn't help but notice that Mr. Morrie Steinberg was once an English professor. It seems to me that Mr. Steinberg's actions, while technically illegal, were motivated by love. If I marry someday, I pray it's to someone like Mr. Steinberg.

In John Connolly's book, The Killing Kind, he wrote, "The nature of humanity, its essence, is to feel another's pain as one's own, and to act to take that pain away. There is a nobility in compassion, a beauty in empathy, a grace in forgiveness."

Perhaps Mr. Steinberg can repay his debt to this community by volunteering his time in our local elementary school, teaching English? I for one would be honored to have him in my class room.
Signed,
Allison Melrose

As luck would have it, District Attorney Edward Stansfield was reading the *Rockport Herald* the day Allison Melrose's letter appeared. He couldn't help but be moved. In short order he spoke to the assistant district attorney assigned to Morrie Steinberg's prosecution.

The various victims were contacted about Morrie's case. Once everyone learned of the motivation behind the thefts, a different tone emerged. One of forgiveness more than retribution.

Walter Higgins's wife, Mary, had actually taken a watercolor class from Esther Steinberg a few years before her stroke. Other victims had seen Allison Melrose's letter to the editor and liked the idea of community service.

Eventually, all the victims agreed not to seek prosecution if Morrie Steinberg agreed to volunteer as an English teacher in the local elementary schools. Morrie was deeply moved by the forgiveness of the people he stole flowers from. He readily agreed to volunteer in the local schools and teach English for the rest of his days.

A new beginning

Morrie began teaching English as an assistant instructor in Allison Melrose's classroom. He'd forgotten how much he loved teaching and felt that he found a new lease on life. As Desmond Tutu wrote, "Forgiveness says you are given another chance to make a new beginning." But more than the teaching, it's what happened next that warmed Morrie's soul and brought tears to his eyes.

Maria Contreras called Morrie and told him to rush over to Oceanview Residential Community. There was something he just had to see. People from all over town had brought something for Esther.

Morrie made his way from the school across town and ran up the steps to Oceanview Residential Community. "Is Esther all right?" he called out to the nurses and Maria.

"Yes, Morrie, she's fine. Go to her room and see her!" Maria said.

Morrie ran into her room and found Esther sitting up in bed, a broad smile on her face. The entire room was completely full of flowers. Freshly cut flowers adorned the shelves, windowsills, her bed, the desk, and in pots and containers all around the floors. Flowers brought from the people of a forgiving, kind community.

"What is this?" Morrie asked as he sat down beside Esther, holding her hand. And for the first time since her stroke, Esther looked Morrie in the eyes and slowly said, "It's...love."

CHAPTER 21

SINS OF THE FATHER

The day she left, I was busy finishing a huge landscape. It was an epic canvas. The pièce de résistance for my upcoming one-man show. I remember talking to her from my studio. Telling her all about my painting. How thrilled I was with the tension in the piece and the vibration of colors.

Of course, I was talking to an empty house. While I was immersed in myself and my art, she had been packing and then quietly left.

Sometimes life makes no sense. Especially the perverse contradictions. Like when one area of your life is blooming beautifully but at the expense of another part of your life.

It's an old and familiar saga. The collision between love and creative passion. Look no further than Frida Kahlo and Diego Rivera. Art and love can fuel a tortured alchemy.

Having it all
There's a sign hanging in my studio bathroom. It says, "Having it all doesn't necessarily mean having it all at once." I always figured it meant I could piecemeal my happiness. You know, have the art success now and work on the love thing later.

I phoned my father and invited him to join me for a beer at our local brewery. I figured a few IPA's were in order, to help me untangle my relationship mess.

Dad doesn't mince words. "It's your own fault, son. I love you, but let's face it; your first love is art. How can she compete with that?"

The short answer? She can't. Who wants to compete with an all-consuming passion? God knows she tried at first. Staying up late until I finished a piece. Going to all those gallery openings. Helping me update my website. But I guess hope doesn't spring eternally, and her patience waned.

I missed her terribly but stayed focused on the upcoming show. Everything was set in place.

I finished all the pieces for my one-man show, shipped them to the gallery, and made my travel arrangements.

And then the phone rang.

"Mom had a heart attack!" my sister, Heather, said. "We're at County General. It's serious. I called Father O'Malley." I could hear the fear in Heather's voice, grabbed my car keys, and raced to the hospital.

Father O'Malley was the local priest in our Catholic church and a friend of the family for many years.

Sins of the father

Dad and Mom divorced when I was thirteen. I think I cried for a month. Dad was an entrepreneur and completely immersed in his work. Mom was always ushering us kids to school and sports and playdates. Dad? He was like a kabuki theater actor. Flitting around in the shadows of our lives. Periodic appearances but never really present. I was mad at him for many years, but in the last few, we started to reconnect.

Father O'Malley spotted me at the nurse's station and pulled me aside, saying, "Your dad is sleeping right now, and your sister went down to the cafeteria. Let's talk."

We strolled over to the chapel and sat down. Father O'Malley faced me, held my hand, and said, "Heather told me the doctors stabilized your mom. She'll require four stents but should be okay." I breathed a sigh of relief. But then Father O'Malley continued, "You know how close I am to your father and mother. But I have to tell you, your father fell victim to his work. It always came first. It's why he's so financially successful. It's why you guys had such a beautiful home on the west side. Let's face it, your dad thrives on the trappings of success. His BMW. His impressive home. But here's the thing. I don't think he's happy. I think he bypassed the simpler things, like family and small pleasures, for his business success."

I looked at Father O'Malley and said, "Why are you telling me this, Father?"

"Because you're just like your father. Sins of the father and all that. You're consumed by your art. And I worry that you've put all your eggs in one artistic basket. It seems to me you wouldn't be alone right now if you found a bit of balance. A space in your life. For her."

Of course, he was right. Father O'Malley was always right. I had driven away the only woman I truly loved, because my art was more important to me.

"How did you know about our breakup?" I asked Father O'Malley.

He smiled and said, "I'm a priest. It's my job to pay attention to my flock." Then he lowered his head and said, "I just worry that once the gallery openings are over, and after the reviews and adulation, you'll have no one to share it all with. Just like your father can't share his success with your mother anymore."

We are what we do
One of my favorite authors passed away recently—Dr. Gordon Livingston. I feel kind of stupid because I've read all his books but obviously didn't absorb anything. Dr. Livingston once wrote, "We

are what we do. Not what we think, not what we say, not what we feel. We are what we do."

What I do is paint. And drive away the people who love me. Maybe Father O'Malley and Dad are right. I've put my art first and everyone else second.

I remember when Dad and Mom got divorced. I was angry and sad. I felt like Dad let us down, and I hated him for a while. But then Father O'Malley told me this: "There's one thing that evil can't stand. And that's forgiveness."

Those words hit me deep and began a thaw in my heart. Before long I reached out to Dad and started a new relationship. To my surprise, he admitted his own mistakes and regrets.

What is essential is invisible to the eye
My one-man show was quickly approaching, and I was getting excited. I knew some influential art dealers and journalists would be there. A few days before the show, I sent an e-mail to my girlfriend. Well, former girlfriend. And part of what I wrote was this:

> My family priest told me the other day that, "What is essential is invisible to the eye. The things that are center stage are rarely the most important." I've made my art center stage for a long time. Everything else was second. But I'm beginning to realize that I need more than art. I need love. I need someone to hug me when I come home. Someone who knows my history. Someone to care for me when I'm sick. Someone to share in my successes and failures.
> What I need is you.

Finally, the night of the one-man show arrived. To my great surprise, Mom recovered enough to attend. Heather and Dad helped her into the gallery. "I'm so proud of you, son," Mom told me. I hugged her for a long time.

Father O"Malley was there. He told me my work must be divinely inspired. God bless him.

There were photographs and interviews and conversations with patrons. It was an amazing night. A night any artist would kill for. Except, something was missing. The woman I most wanted to share it all with.

Near the end of the evening, as the crowd thinned, my agent came over and handed me an envelope. I opened it carefully and read the words, "I need you, too."

My agent smiled and said, "Look above you on the second landing." So I looked up and there she was. Clutching a bouquet of roses and smiling broadly.

I bounded up the stairs and wrapped my arms around her. Told her I loved her. Told her I was sorry. And as Father O'Malley smiled at us from below, I realized that it was possible. I could balance my life between the woman I loved and the art that defined my life. And I felt deeply happy.

CHAPTER 22

WASHING AWAY THE DUST OF EVERYDAY LIFE

She was an elderly widow who lived alone except for her alcoholic son, who occasionally stayed in the downstairs portion of the house.

One night her son got into an argument with his girlfriend and battered her violently. He had been drinking and tended to get abusive. The mother called 911, and the son fled in his vehicle before our police officers arrived.

I was a night-shift sergeant back then. I remember responding to the residence to assist the officers on scene.

The downstairs room where the son stayed was a mess. Liquor bottles on the floor, an overturned chair, dirty laundry. The battered girlfriend had already been taken to the hospital.

As I ascended the outdoor stairs to the main portion of the house, I noticed curious little sculptures hanging from strings. The sculptures were abstract spirals assembled with paper, wood, and twine.

Entering the residence, I observed two of our officers speaking with the woman, who appeared upset and shaken. They repeatedly asked where her son had fled, but she just glanced down and said she did not know.

The silent voice of art

Looking around the living room, I noticed a large bookshelf with many art books. I saw more miniature sculptures around the room. A few abstract paintings hung on the walls.

I could sense the silent voice of art. It was all around me. Outside on the stairs. Inside on the walls and bookshelves. The voice was telling me something about this woman. That creative beauty mattered to her.

I knelt down to her eye level and introduced myself as the sergeant in charge. I told her my first name and said, "There are some amazing little mobile sculptures on the stairs. Did you make them?"

She looked up at me. "Yes," she said quietly.

"And the paintings in here, are those yours, too?" I asked. She nodded yes. "They remind me a bit of Kandinsky," I offered. She brightened up a bit, pleased that I knew a little about art.

I was trying to build rapport with the woman, and it was clear that her art was important to her. She was lonely and disappointed in her son. Artwork was her escape and salvation.

Artwork was everywhere in her home. Her eyes would light up when we discussed art. Artwork clearly made her happy and more hopeful. It was a place she could go to take care of herself and create and feel a little joy.

We talked art and our favorite painters for a while. She pointed out a few more abstract mobiles that she hung in the kitchen.

The patrol guys, who often teased me about my "artistic" side, listened intently. They knew what I was doing. Eventually, I steered the conversation back to her son. "Does he paint?" I asked.

"He used to a little bit when he was…a boy." Then her tears came.

I told her that her son needed help and that his arrest would give the courts a chance to mandate treatment for his alcoholism. Before long, she relented and told me where he had gone. In short order our officers located him, arrested him, and resolved the incident.

Washing away the dust of everyday life

Jan Komski was one of the first Auschwitz prisoners. He produced haunting drawings and paintings of life in the concentration camp.

No doubt part of his purpose was to capture the atrocities and inhumanity. But being an artist, artwork likely provided a way for him to escape the horrors. To have hope.

Komski eventually was liberated and became a US citizen. I read that he passed away in 2002 at the age of eighty-seven and that through his last days he remained alert, lively, courteous, and caring of others. Perhaps artwork was his salvation?

Sometimes artwork is dark and nihilistic, but more often it seems to be celebratory and hopeful. In artwork we see an effort to reveal beauty, hope, and self-expression from the deepest regions of our spirit.

Art washes away from the soul the dust of everyday life.
—Pablo Picasso

The healing power of art

In my father's eighth decade, he descended into the fog of dementia. Such a cruel fate. He was a bibliophile and an intellectual. He once told me that people can weather the physical disabilities of aging. But when the mind goes, life loses meaning.

His dementia was mild at first. Forgetting where he parked his car. Getting lost around town. But then reality began slipping away from him more and more. At least he never forgot my name.

Eventually we had to place Dad in an Alzheimer's and dementia facility. I hated seeing him there, but he was safe, and my mother could no longer care for him at home.

I visited regularly and began to notice something amazing. Whenever the residents would assemble in the art room, they seemed to come alive. Many became truly absorbed in their drawings, paintings, and creative efforts.

For the time that the residents were creating art, they seemed happy. I attribute this to the healing power of art. The same thing happens with sick children in places like Shriners Hospitals. Give them time to make art, and they settle into themselves and are happy for a bit.

That's probably why "the Art of Hope Program" was formed. As stated on their website, "The Art of Hope Foundation works closely with the hospital's Child Life Specialists to develop patient programs that will impact and enrich the children's quality of life and health. The classes are designed to be therapeutic and fun for the children."

The cool part is that the Art of Hope Program utilizes original artwork created by the children. Their graphic arts team makes an electronic copy of the children's artwork.

Products are selected to transfer the children's artwork onto, such as greeting cards, cell phone cases, ties, jewelry, and so forth. The merchandise line created from children's artwork is available for retail or online purchase. Net proceeds benefit Shriners Hospital for Children.

Sick kids are contributing to their own care through their art. How's that for the healing power of art!

Give yourself the gift of art
Scientific studies indicate that art heals. It changes our physiology and attitude from stress to complete relaxation. Fear gives way to creativity and inspiration.

Art and music change our brain wave patterns and affect our autonomic nervous system as well as our hormonal balance and brain neurotransmitters. In short, creating art and listening to music are good for us.

Clearly artwork helped the woman I met with the alcoholic son. Artwork helped my dad and his fellow residents as they navigated the hazy twilight of their lives. And artwork helps sick kids to feel better and have hope.

So keep giving yourself the gift of art, and wash away from your soul "the dust of everyday life."

CHAPTER 23

WHY PEOPLE PAY GOOD MONEY TO BRAND THEMSELVES

Just when the caterpillar thought the world was over, she became a butterfly.

—*Barbara Haines Howett*

Peter Rabbit saved Maria Sanchez's life. It all happened the week after she overdosed on fentanyl, the synthetic painkiller that is eighty to one hundred times stronger than morphine.

Maria's boyfriend Hector scored the drug from a neighborhood connection. He and Maria used to drink heavily, smoke pot, and dabble in methamphetamine. But the night they first tried fentanyl changed everything.

The drug was far more powerful than they bargained for. Hector collapsed on the kitchen floor, and the last thing Maria remembered was giggling at him. She thought it was funny that he couldn't handle his drugs.

The next thing she knew, she woke up in a hospital room. Her brother Efraim was seated next to her, holding her hand. He was the one to tell her that Hector was dead.

Maria cried for a long time. She cried for Hector. She cried for herself. Later, when the police came, she told them everything. Why not? Life for her was over. She had basically given up.

Read me a bedtime story
The third night in the hospital, a nurse came into Maria's room and introduced her to Laura, a county social worker. Laura said to Maria, "Would you let me show you something?"

Maria was wary but said, "I guess so."

Laura fetched a wheel chair and helped Maria into it. She pushed Maria out of her room and down the long hallway. They entered an elevator and descended to the second floor. The pediatric oncology unit.

"Maria, I've read a bit about your history. I know you had it rough. You lost your mom. Your dad split when you were little." Laura looked in Maria's eyes. "The police charged you with being under the influence of a narcotic and constructive possession. For the drugs Hector brought home."

Maria looked down at the floor and said, "I don't care. Jail doesn't scare me. My life is over."

"No, it's not. I think you're a good candidate for our new drug court program. But before we talk about that, I want you to consider doing something for me," Laura said.

"What's that?" Maria asked.

Laura wheeled Maria into the hospital room of Jenny Swanson. "Maria, I want you to meet Jenny. She's ten years old and loves Peter Rabbit," Laura said.

Maria gazed at Jenny's bald head and big brown eyes. Jenny smiled broadly and said, "Hi. Are you going to read me a bedtime story?"

Maria looked nervously at Laura and then back at Jenny. "Uh, yeah, I guess so." With that, Laura handed Maria a children's book. Beatrix Potter's *The Tale of Peter Rabbit*.

Rescued by the sparrows

Skinny and sick from years of drinking and drug abuse, Maria felt like the proverbial ugly duckling. A loser who lost her way in life. Forever wounded by the premature death of her mother and abandoned by her alcoholic father. She felt sorry for herself.

But then she heard Jenny's sweet voice. "Keep reading! What happens to Peter?" So Maria continued with the story. Over the next several nights, Laura would visit and wheel Maria into Jenny's room. To read her *Peter Rabbit*.

Maria's favorite part of the book was when the sparrows came to Peter's rescue. Peter had snuck into Mr. McGregor's garden to nibble on the vegetables. Eventually, Peter was helped by the sparrows who "implored him to exert himself." The lesson? Listen to those who are wiser than we are about the dangers in life.

Another lesson from Peter Rabbit: understand that disobedience has consequences. For some reason, Beatrix Potter's classic children's book spoke to Maria. She loved the beautiful drawings in the book and the life lessons it held.

Before Maria's hospital stay was over, she had begun drawing pictures of little animals. Like Beatrix Potter's drawings in *Peter Rabbit*. One night Laura flipped through Maria's drawings and said, "Maria, you're a talented artist. I have an idea. There's someone I want you to meet."

Everyone has a story to tell

Not long after Maria got out of the hospital she went to court. Thanks to her talented public defender and her cooperation with the police, she was granted probation and required to attend weekly drug counseling. All the while, she continued drawing her

Peter Rabbit–inspired animal drawings. Then one night, the phone rang.

"Hi, Maria, it's Laura. Remember when I told you there's someone I want you to meet? Well, his name is Jeremy Johnson. He's a tattoo artist."

"Uh, I don't think that's a good idea, Laura," Maria said.

"No, no. Jeremy is a phenomenal artist, and he's been clean and sober for twenty years. Just meet with him. I think he'd be good for you." Laura gave Maria his phone number and urged her to call him.

Two days later Maria got the courage to call Jeremy. He was soft spoken and kind and encouraged her to visit his tattoo parlor. The next day she drove to his parlor. All around the walls, there were amazing drawings and sketches. Portraits, animals, fantasy creatures. Jeremy and Maria sat down in his office.

"Laura tells me you like to draw," Jeremy said.

"Yeah. I don't know what happened. After Hector died I met this amazing little girl named Jenny. She's into *Peter Rabbit*. I loved Beatrix Potter's drawings. I've been drawing ever since."

"There's a dude named Nikko Hurtado," Jeremy said. "He's a very successful tattoo artist. He grew up drawing cartoons and studied art for a few years at the Art Center of Pasadena. But then he quit and did construction for three years." Jeremy leaned back in his chair.

"If this is some kind of inspirational speech, I'm not really interested in doing construction," Maria said.

"No, no. One day Hurtado stopped into Art Junkies Tattoo Studio in Hesperia, to see how his friend Mike, a fellow artist, was doing. Mike ended up offering Nikko an apprenticeship, despite the fact he didn't have any experience. The rest was history. Nikko went on to become a superstar in the tattoo industry. He has over three hundred thousand likes on Facebook and a waiting list of clients." Jeremy leaned forward and looked at Maria. "I'd like to offer you an apprenticeship, Maria. Laura showed me some of your drawings, and I think you've got a lot of talent."

"That's very kind of you, Jeremy. But I don't think of tattoos as fine art," Maria said.

"Tattooing is a thousand-year-old art form. It's not the subculture you think it is, Maria," Jeremy said. "One in five Americans has a tattoo. Everyone has a story, Maria. Tattoos are one of the highest forms of individual expression. They tell you volumes about people."

Art is in the eyes of the beholder
Before long Maria was performing tattoos under the guidance and training of Jeremy. Laura would stop by on occasion and encourage Maria. A few of Maria's old friends criticized her new profession, telling her it wasn't art. It bothered her, and she asked Jeremy what he thought true art was.

"Art is in the eyes of the beholder," Jeremy said. "Sure, a lot of people can differentiate between poorly rendered and well-drawn pieces. But who are any of us to define what art is? Look at the English graffiti artist Banksy. He does these distinctive, stenciled pieces of social commentary and dark humor. The guy's first documentary film, *Exit through the Gift Shop*, got him an Academy Award nomination for best documentary."

"Seriously? That's amazing," Maria said. And so she continued on with her work, and over time her reputation grew. Eventually, Maria was able to open up her own tattoo studio. She was famous for her signature brand, a small bunny reminiscent of Peter Rabbit.

Why people pay good money to brand themselves
One day a young woman came into Maria's studio. She had made an appointment months before and today was her big day. She was tall and attractive. As she sat down in the tattoo chair, Maria began preparing her equipment.

A young man flipping through the sample tattoo books saw the young woman getting ready for her tattoo. "Are you sure you want to get inked? I mean, I think I want a tattoo, but I don't know. It's cool and all, but it's also so…permanent."

The young woman smiled at him and said, "Do you know why people pay good money to brand themselves? Because they want to pay tribute to something or someone special."

"Is that why you're here?" the young man asked.

"You could say that. I'm here to get a Peter Rabbit tattoo," the young woman said.

"Yeah, Maria is famous for her rabbits. But why are you paying tribute to a rabbit?" the young man asked.

Curious herself, Maria put down her equipment and said, "Guess I'm curious, too."

The young woman leaned forward a bit and said, "Because when I was a little girl, someone read Peter Rabbit to me, and it made me feel safe. It also taught me to listen to wise people and to walk a straight path."

Maria took a deep breath and glanced down at the young woman's name on the client form. A flash of recognition hit her, and she looked back up at the young woman and said, "Jenny!"

Jenny's eyes welled with tears as she said, "You're my guardian angel, Maria. You read to me when I was sick, and ever since then, I've been in remission. So I had to come to you. I had to get my Peter Rabbit tattoo."

At that moment, as Maria and Jenny held each other in a long embrace, Maria no longer felt like the loser who had lost her way. She no longer felt sorry for herself.

Peter Rabbit had saved her. Her own artwork saved her. And maybe, just maybe, she had saved Jenny.

CHAPTER 24

THE GIFT WRAPPER

Between stimulus and response there is a space. In that space is our power to choose our response. In our response lies our growth and our freedom.

—*Viktor E. Frankl*

Attitude is everything. No matter what life throws at you, you get to decide how to react. But sometimes, your emotions get in the way of reason and sound judgment. Such was the case for Natalie Parker.

As CEO for a leading advertising and design firm, Natalie was a busy woman. Recently back home from a three-day, out-of-state conference with a new client, Natalie was exhausted. It had been a difficult but successful negotiation.

Christmas was only a week away. There had been no time to shop. Leaving her downtown office late that afternoon, Natalie drove her Mercedes along the boulevard toward the city's commerce district. She needed to find some gifts for her family.

Calm before the storm

The skies were beginning to darken as Natalie drove downtown. She was still thinking about work when her mobile phone rang. On the speaker was her sister, Michelle.

"Natalie, welcome home! How did your business trip go?"

"It was a long three days, Michelle, but we got the contract. Come January I'm going to be buried with work." Natalie noticed rain drops on her windshield.

"Well, congrats, Natalie. But I'm concerned that you're working too much. You need to slow down. Oh, and I wanted to ask you about Mom." Michelle let the statement linger, knowing that their mother was a delicate subject.

"I told you, Michelle, I don't want to see her. She's never supported my career. She thinks I'm a bad wife and mother. I'm not gonna have her ruin my Christmas!" Natalie pulled over to the side of the road, too angry to keep driving.

"Ah, Natalie. I know you're angry at her, but she's always been old fashioned. I think she just wants you to spend more time with Tom and Steven." Michelle knew that Natalie loved her husband, Tom, and son, Steven. But she also knew that the rift between Natalie and their mother was eating away at Natalie.

"Michelle, I gotta go. It's almost Christmas, and I'm running out of time! We'll have to talk about Mom later. Talk to you soon." Natalie hung up, closed her eyes, and leaned back in her car seat. It was then that she heard the driving raindrops on the hood of her car, followed by lightning and the crack of thunder.

An unexpected detour

Natalie made it downtown and headed into Nordstrom. The place was a madhouse, bustling with shoppers. Holiday music played throughout the store. Despite the pandemonium, Natalie found gifts for her husband, son, and sister. She already bought gift cards and wine for her friends and a few work associates.

Pleased with her productivity, Natalie got in her car and started the long drive home. The storm was raging now, and some streets were beginning to flood. Natalie drove past repair crews and police officers dealing with power lines and downed tree limbs.

Natalie's husband, Tom, phoned. "Hey, honey, where are you at?"

"Well, I went shopping, but traffic is terrible from the storm. I'm trying to get to the bypass." Natalie noticed a sea of red lights and motorists ahead of her, going nowhere fast.

"The bypass is shut down, Natalie. I heard it on the radio. Some kind of major wreck. You might as well get a coffee somewhere and sit this out for a while. I'll make dinner for Steven, and we'll save you a plate for later." Tom was always thoughtful that way.

"Okay, I'll take Swanson street and hit Starbucks," Natalie said.

Big things come in small packages
Natalie's heart sank as she pulled into the Starbucks. They were closed, due to a power outage. Natalie had time to kill and nowhere to go. It was then that she noticed Lind's Art Store down the street. The lights were on.

"Good evening, can I help you find anything?" the young woman by the cash register said to Natalie. The art store was busy with shoppers.

"Oh, thanks, but I'm just going to browse. I'm sort of stranded because of the storm. I can't get home," Natalie said.

"Well, we've got free coffee in back." The sales woman pointed to the rear of the art store. Natalie thanked her and meandered past shoppers toward the coffee stand.

They say that big things come in small packages, and Natalie was about to discover the truth of that saying. Near the coffee stand stood a gift wrapping station.

There were reams of elegant wrapping paper, ribbons, boxes, and bows, and in the middle of it all was a short, thin, elderly man.

He was smartly dressed in dark slacks, matching suit vest, crisp white shirt, and red tie. His name tag read "Stanley." He sort of looked like an elf.

"There are no strangers here, only friends you haven't met yet," Stanley said as he looked directly at Natalie. Then he added, "William Butler Yeats. I wish it was my line, but a guy my age needs all the help he can get!"

Natalie smiled, immediately disarmed by the charm and warmth of Stanley. Another customer approached Stanley, with some items to be gift wrapped. Stanley smiled, took them, and got to work.

"I used to be an illustrator for Hallmark," Stanley told the customer. "But I retired a few years back. I got Parkinson's, and the tremor in my right hand made it impossible to draw and paint. So, I wrap gifts now! Gift wrapping is an art form, too."

Natalie watched as Stanley expertly wrapped the customer's purchases. She was struck by the elegance and artistry of his efforts.

"Gifts are expressions of love. Gifts need thought. Purpose. How they're wrapped matters. There's no fast way to make a gift look great under the Christmas tree," Stanley said. "We move too fast these days. We miss things. But when we slow down, life resonates more." Stanley winked at Natalie, which made her laugh.

This charming old gentleman somehow radiated a comforting calm and generosity of spirit. So much wisdom and kindness in such a small old man.

Smoothing out the raw edges of life
"I like to use one-hundred-percent-cotton rag paper for wrapping. It feels like cloth. The key to good wrapping is proper measuring and never exposing raw edges. Always fold and smooth them out. And you gotta use double-sided tape, so it's invisible on the outside. Also, you want to crisply crease all the edges and use colorful ribbons. I sometimes like to tie flowers or tree leaves to the ribbon,

so the gift has a touch of outdoor life to it." Stanley handed the beautifully wrapped gifts to the customer, whose delighted smile said everything.

"You're such a chipper fellow, Stanley. Do you ever get angry?" Natalie asked.

"Oh sure, when I was diagnosed with Parkinson's. And when my wife Ethel died. But I came to understand that life is too short to hold on to anger. We miss out on what's important. Life is a lot like gift wrapping. We need to smooth out the raw edges of life." Stanley smiled.

"I want to believe that, Stanley. But sometimes life is just a mess," Natalie said.

"Life is a shipwreck, but we must not forget to sing in the lifeboats," Stanley said.

"That's beautiful, Stanley. Poetic."

"Voltaire. I wish it were mine…" Stanley offered.

But then Natalie added, "But a guy your age needs all the help he can get." And the two of them laughed.

A phone call before Christmas

Natalie picked out a lovely leather day planner and had Stanley gift wrap it. "Is this going to be for someone special?" Stanley asked.

"It's for me, Stanley. Thanks to you, I'm going to reevaluate a few things. Starting with my schedule this coming year. I want to set aside more time for my family."

"What a lovely idea," Stanley said, adding, "Merry Christmas, my dear, Merry Christmas."

Just as Natalie thanked Stanley, her phone rang. It was Tom, letting her know that the bypass was opened up now. "Tom, do you think we could plan a trip in January? Maybe you, me, and Steven could get away somewhere tropical?"

"Uh, yeah. That would be amazing, honey," Tom said. "What brought all this on?"

"The gift wrapper. He's such a darling man. I guess there really are angels on earth, if we slow down long enough to experience them," Natalie said.

"The gift wrapper?" Tom asked.

"Yep, the gift wrapper. I'll explain later. Oh, and, Tom, before I head home, I have one more thing to do. I'll be home in a bit."

The rain had cleared, and Natalie strolled outside and got in her car. She leaned back. Took a deep breath. Exhaled. She gazed at the perfectly wrapped journal she bought. She thought about missed opportunities and the future. And then she picked up her cell phone and called.

It rang a few times, and then, when the voice on the line answered, Natalie said, "Hi, Mama, it's Natalie. I was wondering what you're doing for Christmas?"

CHAPTER 25

MINIMALISM AND THE ART OF CREATIVE SUCCESS

A lot of people are familiar with the talented American actor, director, and producer John Malkovich. He has twice been an Academy Award nominee, capable of performing serious, poignant, and humorous roles.

What a lot of people may not know about John Malkovich is that he is also a serious fashion designer with his own collection. He describes his fashion line as "elegant, discreet, and with interesting details."

In a somewhat tongue-in-cheek yet absorbing short film, Malkovich talks about his passion for fashion design. In one part he says something that a lot of people might relate to:

> I'm always a figure in someone else's dream. I'd really, rather, sometimes make my own figures and make my own dreams.

The questions are, can a world-renowned actor also become a notable fashion designer? Must creative people choose one discipline to achieve greatness? Or can we dance on many stages?

The Renaissance Soul

Margaret Lobenstine, author of *The Renaissance Soul: How to Make Your Passions Your Life*, argues that we should embrace all of our passions. She points out many famous people who were successful in multiple endeavors.

For example, Benjamin Franklin was a successful author, printer, political theorist, politician, freemason, postmaster, scientist, and more.

Leonardo da Vinci was a veritable polymath who successfully pursued inventions, painting, sculpting, architecture, science, music, and more.

Margaret Lobenstine believes that creative people crave variety. They want to "do it all." She believes we should incorporate our many passions into our lives. Ideally, she says we should narrow them down to four interests and pursue those first. We should also find ways to incorporate our passions into our current jobs.

Margaret Lobenstine points to one woman who, later in life, decided she wanted a career in the art world. So she took a clerical position at a museum, which exposed her to curators and other influential people in that industry.

The art of pragmatic juggling

A few years ago, I wrote an article titled "Is Being a Full Time Artist So Great?" In that piece I coined the concept of "pragmatic juggling," which refers to pursuing one's art when and where you can.

The reality is that, despite Margaret Lobenstine's "embrace your passions" philosophy, real life has a knack for getting in the way. For most of us, mortgages and bills don't get paid with watercolor landscapes. The kids don't get braces with a few oil painting sales.

Despite my passion for cartooning, writing, and painting, I stuck it out for twenty-six years in my law-enforcement career.

Why? Because I generally enjoyed the work, and the pay and benefits supported my family.

I pursued my art and writing along the margins of my schedule. But I also distracted myself with other "passions." I regularly trained in the martial arts (jujitsu) and liked to visit bookstores and read new titles.

Additionally, having studied classical piano and performed in two rock bands, I spent many hours playing my baby grand piano and singing.

The point is I had a lot of interests and passions. When not at my police job, I nearly wore myself out trying to pursue all these interests. What's worse, because I'm a perfectionist, I became frustrated at my slow pace of improvement.

I eventually realized that pragmatic juggling is fine if you want to carve out time, away from work, for your hobbies and interests. But what if you want to really excel at something?

The Creative Habit

Twyla Tharp is an American dancer and choreographer who lives and works in New York City. In 1966, she formed her own company, Twyla Tharp Dance. Her work often uses classical music, jazz, and contemporary pop music. Twyla Tharp is also the author of the book *The Creative Habit—Learn It and Use It for Life.*

Twyla Tharp's perspective is different than Margaret Lobenstine's. Tharp argues that you need to pick one thing and practice it daily. By zeroing in on one thing and relentlessly practicing, you stand a much greater chance of success.

As an example, Twyla Tharp points to the composer Mozart. By the young age of twenty-eight, Mozart's fingers and hands were deformed from relentless practice.

Twyla Tharp's book, *The Creative Habit*, offers several suggestions for creative success. One is the importance of *daily rituals*. We must religiously pursue our chosen passion.

Creativity is augmented by routines and habits. Amateurs work when they're inspired, but professionals work every day. Author W. Somerset Maugham put it best:

> I write only when inspiration strikes. Fortunately it strikes every morning at nine o'clock sharp.

Another suggestion from Tharp's book is to "copy" and "read" more. Consider all the art students who travel to museums to copy master works. Doing so teaches volumes about how great artists solved painting problems.

The author Hunter S. Thompson literally copied F. Scott Fitzgerald's *The Great Gatsby* on his typewriter, just to learn the flow, nuance, and pacing of a great novel.

Another area Tharp focused on was the problem of *distractions*. Especially in this day and age of social media, ubiquitous smartphones, busy schedules, and television, it's easy to get side tracked.

This is where the art of minimalism can be a life saver.

The art of minimalism
What's "minimalism"? According to noted minimalists Joshua Fields Millburn and Ryan Nicodemus, "Minimalism is a tool to rid yourself of life's excess in favor of focusing on what's important—so you can find happiness, fulfillment, and freedom."

I discovered minimalism a few years ago and adopted this concept into various areas of my life. I slowly sold or gave away items I didn't need. I let go of relationships that were unhealthy and prevented me from being my best. I reorganized and simplified my office and home studio. I discovered that removing the "clutter" from my life, both physical and emotional, helped me gain clarity and focus on my passion for creating art.

Learning to declutter your home and studio, reducing television, reorganizing your calendar, and politely saying no to people in order to guard your creative time, all help in moving forward and avoiding distractions.

Minimalism is more than pragmatic juggling, because you have to get comfortable with letting go of stuff. Be it physical objects you don't really need or hobbies that are eroding your artistic, creative growth.

When I decided I was serious about becoming a better artist and writer, I gave up the martial arts. I quit being a member of a local service club and reorganized my schedule. I got up earlier and made exercise more of a priority (as it's incredibly important for optimal performance). I cut back on wine parties and nonessential events.

Recently I sold most of my pochade boxes, because they took up space in my studio. Also, I used to stress out deciding which boxes to take out into the field.

Thanks to minimalism, I narrowed down my painting gear to a few lightweight, easy-to-pack equipment. No more stress!

The more you use it, the more you have

The great writer Maya Angelou succinctly sums things up: "You can't use up creativity. The more you use, the more you have."

People define success differently. For some it's all about fame and fortune. For others, it's about self-actualization and personal achievement. When I think about "creative success," I envision reaching new plateaus of artistic excellence that bring me a sense of happiness and fulfillment.

Even the greats were never entirely happy with their work. But they embraced daily rituals. They copied the works of other masters. They fed their minds by reading good books. They fought off distractions and minimized the unnecessary in their lives. If they can do it, so can you.

I don't know if John Malkovich will find the same acclaim in fashion design as he has in acting, but kudos to him for following his heart. While I lean toward Twyla Tharp's view that success comes from picking one thing and practicing it relentlessly, I recognize that people change.

Today's passion might fade, and your heart asks you to turn to something else. I struggle with this sometimes. Am I primarily a writer or an artist? Does pursuing both erode my chances of higher achievement in either discipline? Perhaps.

In the end, consider using minimalism to help you. Strip away the superfluous from your life, if you can, and hone in on your art. Your one, main thing. Remove the distractions, develop daily rituals, and chances are you'll grow and achieve greater creative success!

CHAPTER 26

BIRDS OF A FEATHER

Julia squinted at her painting and stepped back. She looked at the mirror on the wall of her studio. The reflection revealed false junctures in her painting. The mistakes that her eyes had missed.

She returned in earnest to her painting. Readjusting. Modifying values and correcting the aerial perspective. She stood back again and reappraised her efforts.

Something was still wrong. Julia felt a disquietude in her creative heart. Lately, all her paintings left her uninspired. Deep down, she knew that something was lacking.

It was then that she heard the scream in her backyard.

A gift to himself
Edward Larson recently moved to the hills of Los Gatos, California, as a gift to himself. His entire finance career had been in New York, a city he loved dearly. But retirement and the death of his partner, David, changed things.

Edward visited Northern California many times on business trips. Something about the charm of Los Gatos, with its many shops and restaurants, spoke to him.

After retirement and losing David, Edward knew it was time to move and begin a new chapter. Finance may have been Edward's professional life, but his passion had always been art. Particularly, avian art.

He used to draw birds as a boy. He found a sense of tenderness and spirituality in the presence of birds.

His favorite birds of all? Peacocks.

Encounter in the backyard
Startled by the scream, Julia grabbed her cell phone, prepared to call the police. She looked out her rear, sliding glass door, and noticed the hedges moving along the rear of her property.

Just then she saw a slender man in blue jeans and tan polo shirt emerge from the hedges. He had white hair and looked to be about seventy years old.

She cracked the door slightly and yelled out, "Can I help you?"

He waved and shouted, "I'm so sorry to intrude. I'm afraid JJ has gotten away from me. You haven't seen him by chance?"

"No, but I heard a scream," Julia answered.

"JJ does that when he gets excited," the elderly gentleman said.

"Who's JJ?" Julia asked.

"Oh, he's my Indian peacock. I named him JJ because it's short for John James. Sort of a nod to John James Audubon." The gentleman had crossed the lawn and wiped his forehead, clearly a bit winded.

"I really must apologize. I'm your neighbor just beyond the fence line. I moved here last month. My name's Edward. Edward Larson. But my friends call me Eddy."

Stand out from the crowd
Julia realized Eddy was no threat and offered him a glass of lemonade. Eddy readily accepted, and the two sat down in the kitchen to chat.

Julia learned about Eddy's former career in finance and the loss of his partner, David. She told Eddy that she was a professional artist and worked at home in her studio. Eddy's eyes lit up.

"I love art. Especially avian art. David and I collected many pieces over the years. Paintings, sculptures. I'd love to see your work sometime," Eddy said.

"Well, I don't paint birds, but I'm happy to show you my landscapes," Julia offered.

Julia led Eddy to her open studio, with a northern-light-facing window and many landscapes adorning the walls.

Eddy smiled and studiously took in her work. "I see you favor a muted palette. Very strong work. I've always admired tonalist painters. Their restraint and subtle values."

Julia could see that Eddy was knowledgeable about art. Also, he had a kind and gentle disposition. He was easy to talk to.

"I'll be honest, Eddy. Lately I've been feeling stuck. Something's missing. When I compare my work to others in the art magazines, it all looks the same to me." Julia sighed.

"I had an artist friend in New York who went through the same problem," Eddy said as he sat down in one of the studio chairs. "I shared something that seemed to help him. It has to do with standing out from the crowd. I'm happy to share it with you, if you like."

Julia slid a chair closer to Eddy, sat down, and said, "Absolutely."

Peacock wisdom for artists
"Julia, if you want to get the attention your artwork deserves, then you have to stand out from the crowd. It's fine to possess technical skill, but what gets noticed is unique work. Interesting work. Authenticity." Eddy sipped his lemonade and continued.

"What I love about peacocks is their uniqueness. Besides their colorful tail feathers, peacocks also make a loud and distinctive call that demands attention."

"Well, that's for sure! Your JJ scared the heck out of me today," Julia said.

"Peacocks command attention. They're bold. They stand out from the crowd with their beauty. They show their true colors. Do you show the beauty in your art? Does your art command attention? Or do you mask it out of fear? I've met a lot of artists who played it safe," Eddy said.

He looked directly at Julia. "Do you know what makes the feathers of peacocks so brilliant? It's microscopic, crystal-like structures in their feathers that reflect different wavelengths of light. Depending on how they're spaced, the result is bright, fluorescent colors. That's their secret."

"So what you're saying is that I have to find my own secret to stand out. But how do I do that?" Julia asked.

"There's a photographer I like named David Bayles. I memorized something profound he wrote: 'The seed of your next art work lies embedded in the imperfections of your current piece. Such imperfections are your guides—valuable, objective, non-judgmental guides to matters you need to reconsider or develop further.' So, if you want to stand out like peacocks, take a closer look at your current artwork." Eddy sat back, gazing at Julia's landscapes.

"Look there, at the fresh painting on the easel. I see close values, muted tones. But I also see some specks of vibrant color. They don't seem to belong in your picture, but there they are." Eddy pointed at the painting.

"Yeah, I was getting frustrated and tried to experiment with some flecks of color. But now that you mention it, I've been wanting to loosen up and introduce stronger contrast and color," Julia said.

"Unlike the male peacocks, female peahens are a mottled, drab, brown color. They blend into the bushes so that predators can't see them while incubating their eggs. As an artist, you don't want to be a peahen! You don't want to blend in. You want to stand out, Julia," Eddy said with a smile.

Birds of a feather
Suddenly a piercing shriek came from the rear yard. Julia and Eddy jumped up and went to the back of the house. There on the rear patio was JJ, strutting around and pecking at the ground.

Eddy opened the door, walked over, and scooped up his peacock. He turned back to Julia and said, "You know the old saying, 'Birds of a feather flock together.' Birds stick together because there's safety in numbers, Julia. But artists, well, the best seem to stand out. Like JJ, here!"

Julia nodded, amazed at the wisdom coming from this refined, elderly man and his peacock.

"David used to love the Grateful Dead," Eddy added. "He once shared a Jerry Garcia line with me: 'It's not enough to be the best at what you do; you must be perceived as the only one who does what you do.' So, steal a page from my peacock, Julia. Stand out from the crowd. Amplify the clues in your current work. Before you know it, you'll be on your way!"

With that, Eddy thanked Julia for the lemonade, waved, and headed back across the yard. And Julia, amazed by the entire encounter, returned to her studio. Anxious to stop playing it safe. Excited to discover her more authentic, bolder self. Ready to embrace a more vibrant palette of color.

Just like the feathers of an Indian peacock.

CHAPTER 27

WHY COMPARISON IS THE THIEF OF JOY

When I was a boy, my best friend Steven got a new bike for his birthday. It was an awesome bike. It had hand brakes, big fancy tires, and a cool banana seat. Best of all, it had a stick shift in the middle to change gears.

My bike, in contrast, was an old BMX-style Schwinn. It had a small seat, no hand brakes, and certainly no stick shift.

When Steven's father surprised him with the new birthday bike, I could barely contain my emotions. In tears, I hopped on my old Schwinn and rode away from his house.

I overheard Steven ask his dad what was the matter with me. His dad answered, "Oh, I think he's just a little jealous."

Comparison is the thief of joy
President Theodore Roosevelt famously noted, "Comparison is the thief of joy." Whenever we start comparing ourselves to the good fortunes of others, we set ourselves up for unhappiness.

I wrote about this before on my blog. In that article, I recounted my first workshop with the well-regarded painter Scott L. Christensen.

At the workshop, I was surrounded by many accomplished artists. Some were full-timers whose work appeared in multiple galleries. Others were animators and accomplished artists working for design and big-name animation studios.

Then there was me. A full-time police chief and part-time painter. Needless to say, I felt awkward and inadequate. Why? Because I was jealous and a little intimidated by everyone else's skill levels.

Fortunately, Scott Christensen was encouraging and kind. Also, I discovered that my years of drawing and cartooning were an asset in creating the designs and underlying drawings for my paintings.

Best of all, at a critique session after a day of painting, Christensen singled out one of my studies over all the others. He praised the design and execution of the piece. I learned to ignore my jealousies, tap the experience of others, and focus on my own artistic growth. "Just remember," one fellow student said, "it's not a competition."

Envy is ignorance
One of my favorite bloggers, Paul Jarvis, shared an important observation. He wrote, "No one on the Internet is living the life you think they are." In other words, much of what people share is the best of their lives.

The stuff you see on most people's art sites and social-media pages is curated to reflect the best they have. What you don't see are all the failed efforts. The rejected pieces of art, ignored manuscripts, and personal embarrassments.

Ralph Waldo Emerson was right to note, "Envy is ignorance." When we're jealous of others for their success, we display our own ignorance. We only see the end result and not the long road many successful people had to travel.

As the author Mark Manson wrote, "If someone is better than you at something, they probably failed at it longer."

When I look at artists who are further along in my eyes, I have to remind myself that they probably have been at this longer. They probably have been failing forward longer than I have.

Something inside me dies

I used to be a competitive tennis player. I idolized Jimmy Connors and copied the same hard-hitting backhand that Connors was famous for. I played on my high school varsity tennis team along with a buddy of mine.

Whenever my buddy would win more games or tournaments than me, I felt jealous. Instead of being happy for him, I wanted to outperform him.

"Every time a friend succeeds," Gore Vidal admitted, "something inside me dies." Competitiveness is fine up to a point. It can help motivate us and move us forward. But it's a slippery slope. We can devolve quickly to the low road of jealousy.

Some artists experience jealousy when they enter art competitions and their friends do better. As the psychotherapist Diana Pitaru wrote in psychcentral.com, "To create art requires a certain level of introspection and self-connection and when you feel envious and jealous, these capabilities vanish."

In other words, jealousy hurts our artwork. It takes us away from honing our skills and finding our own creative expression.

Similarly, rejection of our artwork can injure us too. Like when you apply for art shows and get turned down.

Pitaru went on to write as follows:

> We feel justified in our envy and jealousy because we take our art very personally and often over-identify with the end results of our craft. The finished product is often the high point through the suffering, anger, frustration, and instability that the creative process can be filled with. And it makes sense, you take pride in the creative outcome because you

see the positive things about yourself that otherwise would elude you. You put your entire self-worth into it and then if someone, more or less directly, expresses disagreement, you get hurt; that is your ego gets hurt.

Life is about not knowing and then doing something anyway

So what are we to do with our petty jealousies and fragile egos? There's no one formula to help reorient our thinking, but perhaps these five suggestions can help.

1. **Embrace gratitude.** It helps to refocus on all that we have achieved. All that we can be thankful for. Yes, there are artists further along than us. But there are others way behind us. Be thankful for your art, personal expression, and the ways it can bring joy to others.
2. **Savor more.** Learn to slow down and enjoy the process. Instead of being in a hurry to conquer that next challenge or artistic hurdle, take some time to savor the joy of your art. The joy of being in the zone and creating.
3. **Put it to work.** Failure may sting, but it instructs. Next time you get rejected from an art show or the publisher says "No" to your manuscript, put that rejection to work for you. Find out where you need to improve. Get as many answers as you can, and then put that knowledge to work for you. Make the necessary changes and watch your ability grow.
4. **Help others.** Don't ask me why but this just works. Every time you let go of petty jealousies and simply help others, it comes back on you positively. I try to help other artists and writers I admire by mentioning them in my articles. This helps draw attention to their work. They often return the favor and share my work. A rising tide lifts all boats.
5. **Risk more.** When I took that workshop years ago with Scott Christensen, I was apprehensive before the plane even

landed. My ego told me I wasn't far enough along to go paint with all those other artists. But I did it anyway. Reasonable risk taking is all about pushing ourselves, trying new things, and learning from the experience. And should you fail in trying something new, refer to number three above.

Author Mark Manson wrote, "Life is about not knowing and then doing something anyway." All the greats felt fear, jealousy, and rejection, too. The difference between them and a lot of dreamers is that they got back up after life knocked them down. They persisted and never gave up.

Stop comparing yourself to everyone else. Ignore those curated images on Facebook. All you're really doing is drowning your joy.

Congratulate your friends and fellow artists who succeed in areas you haven't. Let go of your ego, ask their advice, and learn from their successes. We are all at different stages along our creative paths, but it's a wonderful journey. The trick is to get out of our own way and enjoy it.

CHAPTER 28

THE PRISONER

Sometimes dreams don't come true. The best of plans unravel and life takes you on an unwanted detour.

For Benjamin Foster, that detour led straight to the Barstow County Correctional Center. As most prisoners know, "correctional center" is just a softer word for "prison."

Benjamin used to be a good kid. He played little league and was a decent student. He loved computers and drawing and dreamed of becoming a video game designer.

But things changed. His dad ran off with his secretary. After his parents divorced, Benjamin lived with his mother. Dad infrequently visited and Mom had to work more to make ends meet.

Idle hands are the devil's workshop
Benjamin used to walk home after school and usually had the house to himself. He'd try to get his homework done but often got distracted with television and doodling.

Then one day after school he ran into Sid, a fellow high school student who lived in the neighborhood. Soon the two were inseparable. It wasn't long before Sid introduced Benjamin to alcohol and marijuana.

Benjamin's grades began to slip and arguments ensued with his mother. She lacked the support needed to raise Benjamin.

Marijuana and alcohol led to mushrooms, LSD, rave parties, and then methamphetamine. Benjamin's life was quickly unraveling.

They say idle hands are the devil's workshop. If that's true, then methamphetamine is the fuel that powers the devil's workshop. Benjamin's addiction to meth led to shoplifting, burglary, and crime.

Benjamin's mother was at her wit's end. Her son had been in and out of juvenile hall and even participated in a substance abuse program. But it was all to no avail.

In his early twenties, Benjamin worked part-time at a car wash. The perfect place to deal drugs. Until he got ripped off by some dangerous clients and ended up owing money to his suppliers.

The bank robbery was supposed to be the answer to Benjamin's predicament. How could he know two off-duty cops would be in the bank that day.

The court process played out, and Benjamin's public defender did what she could. In his favor was the fact that Benjamin hadn't use a gun (only pretended to have one) and didn't hurt anyone.

Benjamin's mother cried at sentencing and when her son was escorted out of the courtroom in chains. He was sent to Barstow County Correctional Center. He was no longer Benjamin Foster.

He was now Inmate 27409.

Meeting Rembrandt

Prison frightened Benjamin. Everywhere there were hardened men with tattoos, built-up bodies, and hidden alliances.

The prison noise was relentless. Alarms, slamming doors, arguments, buzzers, screams, and yelling. A concrete hell.

Navigating this new world required effort, luck, observation, bartering, and time. Unfortunately, his four-year sentence provided plenty of time.

Benjamin sought jobs that helped him stay out of trouble and pass the time. His favorite job was working in the prison library.

Years later, he would reflect that the job in the library probably saved his life. Because that's where he met "Rembrandt."

Benjamin's first encounter with Rembrandt was near the rear of the prison library. It was there that Benjamin found this seventy-two-year-old inmate, seated at a desk with several art books opened around him. Also on the desk was a sketchbook filled with amazing pencil drawings.

Benjamin struck up a conversation with the old man and learned that everyone called him "Rembrandt."

"It's funny because I don't even paint," Rembrandt told Benjamin. "The prison budget cut back on paints, so all I've got are sketchbooks and pencils!"

"Yeah, but those drawings are amazing," Benjamin offered.

"I like to copy from the masters. John Singer Sargent. Caravaggio. You can learn so much from these old artists," Rembrandt said.

Old letters and regrets

It wasn't long before Benjamin and Rembrandt struck up a friendship. Rembrandt was sort of like a father to Benjamin. Especially since Benjamin never heard from his deadbeat dad.

"I told you about my robbery, but I don't think you told me your story?" Benjamin cautiously asked Rembrandt one day in the exercise yard.

"Murder. I caught my wife having an affair with a coworker. I suspected it for some time. But then one day, I found her car parked at a motel." Rembrandt shook his head.

"That's terrible. I'm sorry." It was all Benjamin could think to say.

"Back then I was an alcoholic. I was drunk. I kicked in the motel door and lunged at the dude. We fought. He fell; I grabbed this marble statuette in the room and bashed it on the guy's skull. Killed him instantly."

Rembrandt looked at Benjamin and added, "And that was that. The prosecution said it was premeditated. I got thirty years. My wife left me. I had a grown daughter, Sarah, but I lost her too." Rembrandt swallowed hard.

"I'm sorry. What happened to Sarah?" Benjamin asked.

"Oh, mostly time and disappointment, I guess. She used to visit every other month and tell me about life back home. But then she'd just write. For a while, anyway. Now she's down to only Christmas cards."

Rembrandt sat on the yard bench beside Benjamin and looked him directly in the eyes. "Benjamin, it's okay. I'm at peace with it all now. I may only have old letters and regrets left of my family, but they have their own lives to live. I have my art and faith in God."

"I wish I could get where you are, Rembrandt. I used to have dreams, but I'm stuck here for three more years," Benjamin said.

"Well, Benjamin, if you'd like, I'll share with you some hard-earned prison wisdom. I've come up with five life strategies that work both inside and outside prison. I think they can help you." Rembrandt smiled at Benjamin.

"I can use all the help I can get," Benjamin said.

Prison wisdom

The next day in the prison library, Rembrandt opened up a notebook in front of Benjamin. On the page Rembrandt had written his five life strategies:

1. Let go
2. Forgive yourself
3. Own it
4. Emotional maturity
5. Give thanks

As Benjamin gazed at the list, Rembrandt spoke. "When I got to prison, I started to notice something. All the newbies were tense,

An Artful Life

nervous, angry. You could see it on their faces. They were grappling with fear, but more than that. They realized all the things they lost on the outside. Affection, status, approval."

"Yeah, that hit me too," Benjamin said.

"What happens in prison is that we build a mental toughness to survive. Our worlds shrink to television, exercise, reading, maybe chess. But over time we realize we never had much control over our lives. Even on the outside. We learn to let go. The guys in here that learn to let go, they're relaxed. They smile more. *Letting go and acceptance can be freeing.*"

Rembrandt pointed at his list and said, "Number two is forgiveness. For yourself and others. If we keep blaming ourselves and others, it's like emotional quicksand. It will consume us. *Forgiveness opens the door to personal growth.*

"Third is learning to *own your own life*. Too many people blame everyone else. Most of our lives reflect our own choices. Yet people constantly deny this. They blame their spouses, children, parents, bosses."

"Yeah, I'm guilty of that one," Benjamin said. "I still blame my dad."

"Your father has his own demons," Rembrandt said. "You know why I love the library? It's not just the art books. I like to read the classics. All the stuff I should have read when I was young. Greater minds than ours have left wisdom on how to live life, but we're too busy being petty and superficial to go deeper."

Rembrandt returned to the list. "Fourth on the list is *emotional maturity*. How I wish I understood this years ago. Emotional maturity means not making excuses for yourself but taking responsibility and avoiding the shortcuts in life."

"And last but not least," Benjamin said as he read number five, "*give thanks.*"

Rembrandt closed the notebook and said, "Yep, gratitude is frequently forgotten. We grouse about everything. The food. Traffic. Our lousy bosses. We complain with such indignation. Well, how would your petty complaints sound to some guy in the terminal cancer ward? Or to a couple who just lost a child in an accident? Learn to give thanks for your health, your life, and talents."

Benjamin put his hand on Rembrandt's shoulder and said, "Thank you, my friend."

The angels closed their eyes

In his remaining years at Barstow Correctional Center, Benjamin adopted Rembrandt's five life strategies. He studied daily in the library, consuming classic books. He began a course of study in computer science and design.

Rembrandt passed away six months before Benjamin's release from prison. Benjamin mourned his friend's death but felt a deep sense of gratitude for all Rembrandt taught him.

Benjamin wrote letters to people he hurt in his life. He wrote to his father to forgive him. He wrote to Sid and shared Rembrandt's wisdom. He even wrote to Sarah, Rembrandt's daughter, to tell her who her father became.

As Benjamin signed the forms and changed into civilian clothing, he said a quiet prayer of thanks to Rembrandt.

In the prison parking lot, Benjamin's mother said a prayer of her own. A prayer of hope that Benjamin had changed. A prayer for the future.

As Benjamin and his mother drove out of the parking lot, the angels closed their eyes. They said a prayer of thanks and redemption for the prisoner, Rembrandt. For in saving the life of Benjamin, Rembrandt had saved his own soul.

CHAPTER 29

THE SURPRISING VALUE OF ANGER

Do not go gentle into that good night,
Old age should burn and rave at close of day;
Rage, rage against the dying of the light.

—*Dylan Thomas*

When Bob Lee called me several years ago, I figured it was just another work-related matter. As chief of police in my community, I was accustomed to calls from the district attorney.

"Hi, Bob, I hope we didn't mess up an investigation or something," I said over the phone with a chuckle.

"Nope, not at all," Bob answered. Then there was a pause. Pauses always make me uncomfortable. Especially from the district attorney.

"John, you're one of the most creative, artistic guys I know." Bob paused again, clearly buttering me up.

"The county treasurer just backed out, and you're the perfect guy to bail me out," Bob continued. He added, "It's a silly little thing, really, but something to cross off your bucket list."

I didn't have a bucket list. Bucket lists are about achieving life goals before you kick the bucket. I didn't plan on kicking the bucket anytime soon, so I figured not having a bucket list insulated me from the inevitable.

"So, Bob, what's this 'silly little thing' you want me to do?" I asked warily.

"I want you to dance in the *Nutcracker* with me this Christmas," Bob answered.

"Dance in the *Nutcracker*? Like…ballet?" I said.

"It's a silly little thing, really," Bob replied.

A wakening experience
A recent article in the *Wall Street Journal* chronicled how "retirement communities and colleges are teaming up so older learners can audit classes."

The article introduces Henry Nusbaum, who will soon be turning 103 years old. Henry is taking a college class on medieval history. He wears a head set to hear the instructor better and keeps extra pens in a pocket on his walker.

What struck me in the article is what Henry had to say about his intellectual curiosity:

> This, to me, is a wakening experience. I find the way to continue to enjoy life is to live it, to be involved, to participate in as many programs as I could gracefully, without interfering.

Henry lives in a retirement community where he and several other residents in their late eighties and older can audit classes for free at the adjacent college.

The article noted the "popularity of higher education in the later decades of life. The National Center for Education Statistics counted more than sixty-six thousand people over the age of sixty-four enrolled in degree-granting postsecondary institutions in 2013, the most recent year for which the figures were available."

There are similar arrangements around the country, whereby older folks can audit college classes for free. They don't have to take the tests or do the homework, but some do.

Beyond the enrichment and intellectual stimulation these classes provide for the elderly, another plus are the cross-generational conversations that occur with the younger students.

Clearly, the zest for life and intellectual engagement doesn't have to evaporate in old age. Some make the decision that they're simply not done yet. There is more to learn and experience.

I've seen two kinds of spirits in the assisted living community where my mother lives. The first are the ones who have given up. There's no more fight left in them.

The second group is the spirited ones. Often they're angry. They've still got things they want to do. Stuff they want to say and learn.

They're the ones who "refuse to go gentle into that good night." They've decided to tap into their anger and use it as fuel to move forward.

Weekends with Drosselmeyer and the Sugar Plum Fairy
The last thing I wanted to do was perform in the county's *Nutcracker* production. My job left precious free time for family, exercise, and artwork. Bob told me that that there would be several rehearsals each month leading up to the big production.

I liked Bob and didn't want to disappoint him. I also knew it was important to have good relations with the District Attorney's Office. Begrudgingly, I agreed.

It wasn't long before I regretted it. The rehearsals turned out to be every weekend leading up to the big night. Every Saturday for a few hours, I had to go to rehearsal.

I got to know the performers playing Drosselmeyer and the Sugar Plum Fairy. They taught us how to apply stage makeup and dance. The teasing from the guys at the police department was relentless.

I started to resent the commitment that I had signed on to. I quickly got tired of the grief I received from my coworkers. Even my family started to complain about the time away.

The experience was making me grumpy and angry. I felt a bit put upon and irritated that I had no time left for my painting and writing. But then I decided to channel my anger. I decided that I'd show everyone, by willing myself to do a great performance. "Like it or not, I'm going to make this a positive experience," I told myself.

Keeping PACE with my artwork

I retired from my law-enforcement career last December. Finally, I'd have the time to start painting more. Sometimes, however, things don't go as planned.

My writing schedule for my blog, newsletter subscribers, and other websites had increased substantially. To support my wife (a hospice nurse), I took over more household duties like laundry, vacuuming, and making dinner. I was also exercising more. But I wasn't painting much.

I adjusted my morning schedule and finally started painting, but the work was rusty. Stale. I could tell I wanted to change things up and develop a new direction for my art. Unfortunately, I was in an artistic funk.

A reader of my blog was kind enough to send me a discount coupon for the upcoming Plein Air Convention and Expo (PACE) this April in San Diego. And you know what? I considered not going.

I was angry that my painting was not further along. I thought maybe I should just use the time in April to do a ton of studies.

But then I started to channel my anger. "If you're unhappy about your work, do something about it. Stop making excuses. Go to the convention, get r-inspired, and stop this whining," I told myself.

So, I'm signed up to attend the convention and excited to invest in my artistic growth. All because my anger motivated me to take action. I guess sometimes the best way to keep "pace" with your artistic growth is to channel your anger and frustration into something productive.

The surprising value of anger
Here's the thing about anger. It can be destructive. I read somewhere that "anger is a hot coal you throw at the person you're angry with. But you still burn your hand."

Unresolved anger can lead to health problems and endless unhappiness. But the reality is that we're all human. Sometimes we get angry. At ourselves, other people, or circumstances. What matters is what we do with that anger.

The surprising value of anger is that, when properly channeled, it can fuel positive action and solutions.

Remember my district attorney friend, Bob Lee? He died two years later, in his early fifties, of cancer. Looking back, I was so glad I channeled my anger about those weekend *Nutcracker* rehearsals into seeing my commitment through.

After opening night at the *Nutcracker*, the entire cast celebrated backstage with champagne. I remember Bob was beaming as he looked at me and said, "Wasn't that great? Cross it off your bucket list, John!"

It might have been a "silly little thing," but fortunately I was able to channel my anger. I stayed the course and danced in the *Nutcracker*. It's something that I'll always cherish.

I suspect my experience at the Plein Air Convention and Expo this April will also be a positive experience. Much like taking college classes is for a 103-year-old gentleman who still wants to learn.

So, whatever you're angry about, channel it into something productive. Work toward that solution, and I think you'll be surprised and happy with the results.

CHAPTER 30

WHY I STEAL LIKE A THIEF AND YOU SHOULD TOO

What has been will be again, what has been done will be done again; there is nothing new under the sun.

—*Ecclesiastes 1:9*

I steal like a thief. In fact, I've been doing it for years. I used to feel kind of bad about it, but I'm over it now. Why? Because it has helped me grow. And, I'm in good company.

I was in law enforcement for twenty-six years, so admitting to thievery is a bit contradictory. However, the kind of stealing I'm talking about is not illegal. As long as you manipulate what you stole into something all your own.

For a case in point, I give you Richard Diebenkorn.

Masters across the decades
The *Wall Street Journal (WSJ)* recently ran an excellent article, "Masters across the Decades," about the painters Richard Diebenkorn and Henri Matisse.

Diebenkorn idolized the work of Henri Matisse. In 1943, when Diebenkorn was an art student at Stanford, he came across his first Matisse painting. From then on, Diebenkorn sought out Matisse's work. He was deeply affected and influenced by it.

As the article states:

Again and again, Diebenkorn (1922–1993) would create drawings and paintings whose structure, palette, light, fluidity and sense of place profoundly embraced Matisse.

There's nothing wrong with idolizing another artist. There are many painters and writers who channel the work of their heroes.

Diebenkorn borrowed liberally from Matisse's palette, designs, and more. But, as the *WSJ* article notes:

Always, though, "he was able to make them new," as scholar John Elderfield writes in the catalog for Matisse/Diebenkorn, a stunningly beautiful display here at the San Francisco Museum of Modern Art.

The San Francisco Museum of Modern Art exhibition intersperses forty paintings and drawings by Matisse with sixty by Diebenkorn. The influence of Matisse on Diebenkorn is undeniable, yet Diebenkorn evolved in his own right.

Diebenkorn moved from abstraction to lush streetscapes, still lives, figurative work, and then back to abstraction. The *WSJ* article adds:

Diebenkorn had changed dramatically. No longer making the energy-filled abstractions of his youth, or the sumptuous figurative works of his middle years, he had evolved into a painter of quiet, peaceful, thoughtful works.

Other artists, like Cezanne, Mondrian, Bonnard, and Hopper all influenced Diebenkorn. Of course, Matisse was Diebenkorn's loadstar. He may have stolen from them all, but he transcended them and emerged as the artist we celebrate today.

Steal like an artist
New York Times best-selling writer Austin Kleon describes himself this way: "I'm a writer who draws. I make art with words and books with pictures."

A while back I picked up Kleon's popular book, *"Steal Like an Artist: 10 Things Nobody Told You about Being Creative."* The little book is packed with all sorts of helpful insights.

For example:

> We learn by copying. We're talking about practice here, not plagiarism—plagiarism is trying to pass someone else's work off as your own. Copying is about reverse engineering…Remember: Even The Beatles started as a cover band.

When I was a teenager, I used to copy the paintings of fantasy artist Frank Frazetta. I loved the way he exaggerated anatomy and connected shapes in his work. By aping his style, I learned a lot about design and color.

With my cartooning I leaned heavily upon the work of Jeff MacNelly, a three-time Pulitzer Prize winner for editorial cartoons. I loved his lush detail and superb crosshatching. My cartoons today still bear his influence, but I'm beginning to see more of my voice now.

Artwork is a lot like cursive handwriting (are schools teaching it anymore?). Students are taught the same shapes, loops, and the like. But over time everyone develops his or her own unique hand. So it is with art.

The key is to keep making art. You need to do a lot of it in order to allow your own authentic expression to emerge. As Austin Kleon says, "Don't wait until you know who you are to get started."

See like your heroes
Stealing (maybe "borrowing" is a softer term) from other artists helps us learn how they solved problems. It's why so many art students go to museums and copy the masters. It also helps us build technical skills necessary to (eventually) free our own unique voices.

Austin Kleon put it this way:

> You are the sum of your influences…Your job is to collect good ideas. The more good ideas you collect, the more you can choose from to be influenced by…Seeing yourself as part of a creative lineage will help you feel less alone as you start making your own stuff…You don't want to look like your heroes, you want to see like your heroes…That's what you really want—to internalize their way of looking at the world…It is the act of making things and doing our work that we figure out who we are.

Kleon encourages us to "be curious about the world in which you live…Always be reading…Don't worry about doing research. Just search." I think that's pretty good advice.

The not-so-secret formula for becoming known
In Kleon's best-selling follow-up book, "*Show Your Work! 10 Ways to Share Your Creativity and Get Discovered,*" he advises us:

> If there was a secret formula for becoming known, I would give it to you. But there's only one not-so-secret formula that I know: Do good work and share it with people. It's a

two-step process…Not everyone will get it…So get comfortable with being misunderstood, disparaged, or ignored—the trick is to be too busy doing your work to care.

One of the benefits of being an unknown artist, according to Kleon, is that you can "enjoy your obscurity while it lasts…There's no pressure when you're unknown. You can do what you want. Experiment. Do things just for the fun of it. When you're unknown, there's nothing to distract you from getting better."

Best-selling author Jeff Goins put it this way: "Creativity is not about coming up with something new and original. It is about borrowing ideas from a variety of sources and re-assembling them into a better or at least different package."

You don't have the right to remain silent

There may be nothing new under the sun, but we are still inspired by every beautiful sunrise and sunset.

Henri Matisse was the wind beneath Richard Diebenkorn's wings, yet Diebenkorn managed to chart his own flight path.

The Pulitzer Prize–winning cartoonist Jeff MacNelly influenced a generation of cartoonists with his sketchy style. Yet he himself was influenced by the animator and comic-strip artist Walt Kelly (who drew "Pogo") as well as the editorial cartoonist Pat Oliphant.

Fantasy artist Frank Frazetta was so influenced by the comic artist Hal Foster (who drew the *Prince Valiant* comic strip) that he even mimicked Foster's signature. Yet Frazetta, just like Richard Diebenkorn and Jeff MacNelly, found his own way and succeeded.

It's okay to steal like a thief. Copy the masters and your heroes. Heck, even the great John Singer Sargent copied the works of other masters. But there's one caveat, and it is this: you don't have the right to remain silent.

If you steal from other artists, you must acknowledge it. Give them credit. In this way, you honor your influences.

Finally, you can't stop when your work resembles the ones you admire. You have to keep pushing and digging deeper. Sooner or later, your own beautiful sunrises and sunsets will emerge.

CHAPTER 31

THE OVERLOOKED BENEFITS OF RUTHLESS EDITING

Kill your darlings, kill your darlings, even when it breaks your egocentric little scribbler's heart, kill your darlings.

Stephen King, On Writing: A Memoir of the Craft

One of my favorite art books is Richard Schmid's *Alla Prima—Everything I Know about Painting.* On page twenty-five we find a photo of Schmid's unfinished portrait, *Princess.*

According to the text adjacent to *Princess,* Schmid describes how he was "blithely" completing this "rather academic" portrait when his wife Nancy intervened. Schmid adds:

> She made me stop at this point, when my painting was strongest, leaving drips and bold strokes.

Richard Schmid often declares a painting finished even though portions of it clearly are not. He does this because sometimes the bones of a painting say more than a fleshed-out piece.

Ever did a preliminary sketch for a larger painting and then struggle to duplicate the freshness and charm of your preliminary sketch?

Sometimes less is more, and we overcomplicate things through needless addition. It often leads to overworked paintings that fail.

The same principle is true in our lives. We overcomplicate things through needless addition. And then we fail.

On Distant Ground

When I studied landscape painting with Scott L. Christensen, he often talked about "orchestrating" a painting. Moving and adjusting the various parts into a cohesive whole.

Scott also talked about "subordinating" or playing down certain areas of a painting. Much like an opera, if the entire performance is solos and high notes, it would become monotonous.

We need quiet spaces to rest our ears. We need white spaces to rest our eyes. Good designers understand this. When the design gets too busy, you lose people. Their attention span wanes because their brains crave simplicity.

I'm lucky to have a copy of Scott Christensen's first book, *On Distant Ground*. In the book, Scott shares the following observation:

> Maybe you're standing in a place where the sky and the mountains are very dramatic; the trees have incredible color and the water is vibrant. You have to decide what you want your painting to be about, render that element the most important, and then paint everything else to support it.

I think a lot of us are standing on distant ground. Out there in the wilderness a bit, trying to find our way. We got lost in the minutia. The underbrush of life.

Part of the reason we lose our way mirrors why we fail with some of our paintings. *Because we overdo it.* We put too much into it. We haven't learned how to "subordinate" various aspects of our lives.

Scott said that you "have to decide what you want your painting to be about." Well, we have to decide what we want our life to be about, too.

The ruthless editor
I used to pay a professional copyeditor to read my stuff and shred it. I'd write up a piece that I thought was the bomb. I'd e-mail it off to this guy. The next day he'd reply, and my article would be torn apart.

I learned that most adverbs are needless adornments. I learned to shorten paragraphs and craft more compelling headlines and subheadings. In short, I learned the value of ruthless editing.

Fast forward a few years. I discovered the whole minimalist movement. I began reading about people who discovered that there was more to life than endless consumerism.

I learned that most people's financial problems stem from too much house, too much car, and too much retail therapy. Their things end up owning them.

I started looking at my own life and where I could downsize and simplify. I may not be a hardcore minimalist, but I have benefited from "editing" the parts of my life that needed to be "subordinated."

Just like in painting and good writing, the art of ruthless editing often leads to a better product. A better life.

What matters most?
According to an article in *Journey Christian News*:

> Editing is eliminating that which is nonessential so the essential can show through. Lin Yutang wrote, "The wisdom of life consists in the elimination of nonessentials." When we stop trying to do it all, stop saying yes to everyone, then

we can make the highest contribution toward what really matters. Editing is not about getting more things done; it is about getting the right things done. It does not mean doing less for the sake of less. It is about making the wisest possible investment of our time and energy in order to operate at our highest point of contribution by doing only what is essential.

A guiding principle we should ask ourselves with each piece of art, and with our lives, is this: "What matters most?"

For me, I've whittled that question down to four pillars I try to focus my life around. They are the following:

1. **Health.** I exercise, eat responsibly, and get enough sleep. Without our health, it's hard to get the most out of life.
2. **Family.** Family is an essential ingredient to a fulfilling life. It doesn't have to be blood relations. For some folks, it's close friends or even their pets. But love matters in a well-rounded life.
3. **Faith.** This relates to believing in something greater than yourself. For some, it's a particular religious faith. For others, it's a feeling of oneness with nature. Getting outside of yourself helps you focus on others and the world around you.
4. **Passions**. Without art and creative expression, I'd be an unhappy guy. So, I've ruthlessly edited my life to amplify my passions. I've said no to commitments that keep me away from the artistic passions that bring me joy.

The article in *Journey Christian News* shared the following observation:

> As people age and approach their final breath, many of them discover the power of editing. They recognize what

matters most, what will stand the test of time, and what is essential. Wouldn't it make more sense to edit our lives now, determining what is most important, rather than waiting until the end of our life?

Do yourself a favor, with your art and life. Take a moment to sit down and mentally edit. For your art, ask yourself what you can edit to possibly enhance the work.

For your life, examine the things that are inessential. Ask yourself what life would look like if you edited those things out. Yes, some things are beyond our control. But you'd be surprised how much we do have dominion over.

The overlooked benefits of ruthless editing are better artwork and a simplified, more meaningful life. So grab a red pen, slash away at the unnecessary, and start creating the artwork and life you always dreamed of.

CHAPTER 32

IF YOU WANT TO BE A FULL-TIME ARTIST, READ THIS

Ever since I was a kid, I loved drawing cartoons. At first, I did cartoons just for my family and friends. Then I caricatured my schoolmates, teachers, and even strangers. Birthdays and holidays were opportunities for me to craft homemade cartoon cards.

In high school I began reading editorial cartoons in newspapers. Unlike comic strips, editorial cartoons were more ornate, detailed drawings. I was hooked. Before long, I became the editorial cartoonist for my high school newspaper.

I continued my editorial cartooning in college, where I lampooned campus life and political issues. After college and graduate school, I became a police officer but still carved out time for cartooning. I became a part-time editorial cartoonist for two local newspapers.

After a few years, I was known around town as the "cartooning cop." I joined the Association of American Editorial Cartoonists and attended their annual convention in Minnesota. As much as I enjoyed my law-enforcement career, I started to fantasize about becoming a full-time editorial cartoonist.

One day a staff editorial cartoonist position opened up at a sizable newspaper in New York. I knew that newspapers were starting to struggle and cartoonist positions were precarious. But I still applied for the position, sending a complete packet with samples of my work, cover letter, and résumé.

The rejection letter came about three weeks later. I was both disappointed and strangely relieved. Deep down, I knew my police career offered an excellent health plan, decent salary, and career security. Three things the cartoonist position could not guarantee.

Sometimes the things we wish for are not what's best for us. We just don't see it at the time.

Careful what you wish for
That editorial cartoonist position I applied for in New York? It was eliminated. Newspapers increasingly laid off their staff editorial cartoonists. It was more affordable for papers to purchase syndicated cartoons.

Had I gotten what I wished for back then, I would have been unemployed with few prospects for other cartoonist positions. Fortunately, I didn't get the position. Instead, I spent twenty-six years in law enforcement and retired with a pension and excellent health benefits at the age of fifty-two.

During those working years, I became a "pragmatic juggler." I found the time to continue cartooning, doing cartoons for law-enforcement publications. Later, I took up landscape painting and fell in love with fine art.

Midway through my police career, I started to fantasize about life as a fine artist. I took a few workshops and got to meet some full-time artists. Their lives seemed idyllic. Romantic. Except there's always more to the story.

The devil's in the details
A few years ago, I wrote an article titled "Is Being a Full Time Artist So Great?" Here's an excerpt:

Yes, we all fantasize about living the artist's life. Painting all day, attending openings, teaching workshops and selling all our work to adoring patrons. Sounds nice. But talk to a full time, working artist. It's a tough road. Galleries are demanding. Supplies are expensive. The business side of art, with all its promotion and marketing, can be exhausting. Sometimes all of these pressures steal the very joy out of making art. Yes, there are a few artists who seem to be living the fantasy. But there are many other professional artists who are really struggling.

In an article titled "How Being a Full Time Artist Will Change Your Life," writer Carolyn England had this to say:

> You make a lot of sacrifices. It's hard work running a business, and you may find yourself on the road away from your family, or working many long, thankless hours. Everyone else gets paid first—your suppliers, show promoters, your employees, the government. Get used to it. Everybody you know thinks you have the coolest job ever and you get no sympathy.

The devil is in the details, as the above quotes illustrate. The rest of the story is simply this: being a full-time artist is hard work. Full-time artists have to be full-time business people, too. That means dealing with inventory, clients, contracts, expenses, taxes, and more.

The upside is that a full-time devotion to one's craft accelerates artistic growth. That's why so many full-time professional artists tend to paint better than hobbyists and part-time artists. It's why they're in the magazines more, teach workshops, have collectors, and sell higher-priced pieces.

The downside is the irregularity of income, business headaches, stylistic accommodations for market realities, difficult clients, endless marketing, and more.

Despite the many challenges and realities of being a full-time artist, this doesn't mean you shouldn't dive in. You just need to do it with your eyes wide open.

How bad do you want it?
A lot of people are in love with the idea of something more than the reality. For example, as a boy I studied classical piano. Later, I became a keyboardist and singer in a few rock bands. I dreamt of being a famous musician someday.

The only problem was that I didn't want it bad enough. The fame and money sounded great but not the travel, hustle, sacrifices, and risks. Country music artist Tim McGraw wrote a song titled "How Bad Do You Want It." Here're a few lines of the lyrics:

> Are you eating, sleeping, dreaming
> With that one thing on your mind?
> How bad do you want it?
> How bad do you need it?
> 'Cause if you want it all
> You've got to lay it all out on the line

Art-business consultant Maria Brophy, in her article "Do You Have What It Takes to Be a Full Time Artist?" outlined the mind-set and qualities that successful, full-time artists share. They

- have a long-term vision of what they want out of work and life;
- are 100 percent committed to bringing that vision to life;
- work on their art every day; and
- invest in coaches, attorneys, trade shows, and courses so that they continually up-level their business.

Brophy then outlined the mind-set and qualities of artists who may not be ready to dive into a full-time art career. They

- are not clear on what they want out of life or out of their art business;
- are not willing to make a commitment to the business;
- are not willing to be flexible or try new things;
- are not willing to learn how to price art properly or doesn't care about money;
- have too many responsibilities (i.e., caring for children or sick family member or anything that takes you away from the business for large chunks of time); and
- have no interest in learning the business end of the art business.

A rose by any other name would smell as sweet
In the end, I think we spend too much time on titles and labels. The evolution of the Internet and technology today has changed the nature of many professions. Fewer and fewer people toil their whole career in one place, doing just one thing.

There is an increasing, transient nature to employment today. More and more knowledge workers act as free agents, often working for many vendors, clients, and companies. In short, people are wearing more hats.

Does it really matter if you're a "full-time" versus "part-time" artist? One may not be better than the other, just different. I know in my case, I'm thankful for my police career.

I got to pursue my art on the side and retired young enough to paint full-time now. Best of all, my pension affords me the freedom to paint what I want, not what a gallery or trend dictates.

Writer Brian Sherwin addressed this issue in a blog post, titled "Don't Fall for the Part-Time vs. Full-Time Artist Trap." Here's what Brian wrote:

> Here's the thing about the part-time artist vs. full-time artist issue: I don't see the point in mentioning part-time

or full-time when discussing the status of an artist. It just seems like a bunch of chest-thumping. The artist is an artist, period. Not to mention that several famous artists embraced multiple directions outside of the art studio. Is Shepard Fairey a "part-time" artist because he is deeply involved with his clothing line? Was Warhol a "part-time" artist because he continued to do illustration work on the side? Was Richard Serra a "part-time" artist when he helped operate a professional moving service? I don't think anyone will describe these individuals as "part-time" artists.

I think Brian hit the nail on the head. If the muse of creativity whispers in your ear, then you're an artist. Whether that's full-time or part-time probably doesn't matter.

In Shakespeare's play *Romeo and Juliet*, Juliet says the following to Romeo:

What's in a name? that which we call a rose
By any other name would smell as sweet;

Juliet is telling Romeo that it doesn't matter if he is from her rival's house of Montague. In other words, the names of things do not affect what they really are.

If you create art, then you're an artist. For some, it's a calling so deep they have to dive in full-time. If so, do it with your eyes wide open. For others, they dance with the muse while caring for their family or holding down a day job. Both approaches bring their rewards and disappointments.

No approach is wrong or right, just different. In the end, the most important thing of all is to enjoy every minute of your art. For it is truly the gift that keeps on giving.

CHAPTER 33

THIS IS WHY ART WILL NEVER LET YOU DOWN

There is an assisted living center in my town that I often visited as a young police officer. Our police department frequently received 911 calls for medical emergencies, thefts, and other incidents. The police and fire staff referred to the center (sadly) as "God's waiting room," since most of the residents were elderly and in poor health.

One day I responded to a call regarding a very emotional old gentleman who was refusing his medication. The center staff felt that a police officer would encourage more cooperation.

Upon my arrival I was led to the gentleman's apartment. The staff member knocked on the door, and a tall, slender man in his eighties emerged. The staff member introduced me to the gentleman and said that I was there to help.

The shadows of reality
The old gentleman's eyes were red, and he had a habit of bursting into tears for no apparent reason. I was told he had mild dementia. He knew his name and where he was but was clearly living in the shadows of reality.

Looking around the room, I noticed that he was an artist. There was a French easel set up near a window and paintings were all around the room. The gentleman was an accomplished painter, as his still lives and landscapes were all well designed and executed.

"They tell me you don't want to take your medication," I said to the gentleman. He eyed me and moved over to his easel where he took up his brush and resumed painting. "Does the medication make you ill?" I asked. The gentleman told me no, he just didn't feel like taking his medicine.

He slowly opened up a bit about his wife, whom he lost a few years ago. Then he burst into tears again. "You must really miss her," I said. He wiped his eyes and looked at me, nodding affirmatively. His eyes had the thin glaze of cloudiness that age brings. But they were penetrating and intelligent, despite his dementia.

I complimented him on his paintings but he didn't respond. He just continued to paint intently, almost as if I were no longer in the room. After a bit I told him that I was sorry he lost his wife, but at least he still had his art. With this he stopped painting, looked at me, and said, "Yes, a loyal companion."

What stories they must have held
Eventually the assisted living staff member returned, and the gentleman finally agreed to take his medication. I wished him well and returned to my patrol duties.

There would be many more trips to the assisted living center during my patrol years. Sometimes to render assistance but frequently to handle death calls.

I remember numerous times when I would wait for the coroner to arrive. Often it would be in the middle of the night. Amid the silence, I'd look around at the photos in the apartment. Pictures of grandchildren, family, and friends. Small collectibles from a long life and travels. I frequently wondered what stories they must have held.

I think it was the writer Christopher Hitchens who said of life's slow unraveling that it "all comes down to a bed." When we are old and infirm, we languish in a bed, in a room, before crossing over the vale.

Ideally, it would be nice to have some of the things that mattered most to us nearby. The majority of the old souls who departed at the assisted living center were fortunate enough to die with their pictures and mementos nearby.

Art promotes healthy aging
An article in the *New York Times* titled, "Using the Arts to Promote Healthy Aging," notes that "the arts in their myriad forms are enhancing the lives and health of older people—and not just those with dementia—helping to keep many men and women out of nursing homes and living independently. With grants from organizations like the National Endowment for the Arts and the National Institute on Aging, incredibly dedicated individuals with backgrounds in the arts have established programs that utilize activities as diverse as music, dance, painting, quilting, singing, poetry writing, and storytelling to add meaning, joy, and a vibrant sense of well-being to the lives of older people."

The *New York Times* article goes on to introduce us to Mr. Hurlburt, who "once made a living as a sign painter, now decorates rooms at the Burbank Senior Artists Colony, a retirement facility where he lives, with lovely oil paintings he creates from pictures he finds in magazines and books. Mr. Hurlburt regularly attends classes on various art forms at the residence where, he told me, 'I'm always learning something new.'"

There is a documentary that came out a while back, titled "Do Not Go Gently—The Power of Imagination in Aging." In it we meet 109-year-old Leo Ornstein, who defies convention.

A Russian-born composer and pianist who in the early twentieth century was a leading figure of the American avant-garde movement, Leo Ornstein was viewed as a radical composer.

In the documentary we learn how a full artistic life changes over time. As Ornstein stated, "One has to be very careful not to become obsessed with one's own style." In his late nineties, Ornstein composed some his most personal and romantic music, though it was colored with grief.

The documentary shows us that, even in his hundreds, Ornstein is honest. As the film's director points out about Ornstein, "He does not have the answers. He does not know the meaning of life. And he admits there may not be a God." And yet, to the very end, Ornstein had his music.

A loyal companion

I'm no longer that young patrol officer handling death calls in our local assisted living center. After twenty-six years I have retired from law enforcement to focus on my art and writing. Yet I still visit the center, because my mother lives there now.

When I bring her groceries each weekend, I walk past her collection of photographs and mementos. But these photographs and mementos are familiar, because I am in the pictures with our whole family.

Along the walls are a few of my father's oil paintings. To this day, my mother gazes upon them and speaks fondly about my father. Dad may have left us in 2004, but his spirit lives on in those paintings. This is the power of art.

It has been many years since I helped the old artist gentleman in the assisted living center. I don't remember when he passed away, only that it wasn't long before his room was inhabited by a new resident. But I figured when his time came, he was surrounded by his paintings, his easel, and his brushes.

He was surrounded by his art. His "loyal companion."

Whenever I reflect on that experience, I realize just how special it is to be an artist. To be blessed with the fire of creativity in our hearts. It is a gift that stays with us, like a loyal companion, to the very end.

This is why I know that art will never let you down.

CHAPTER 34

THE SECRET TO A HAPPY MARRIAGE

The elderly couple were holding hands in the hospital room when the nurse entered. The nurse was experienced, and she particularly enjoyed caring for older patients.

She gazed at the couple and was moved by the way they tenderly held hands and spoke to one another.

When the gentleman's wife ended her visit and left, the nurse respectfully asked, "May I ask how long you have been married?"

He answered, "Sixty happy years."

With that the nurse said, "I must ask you, what's your secret?"

The old gentleman smiled, leaned back, and said, "AREA, young lady."

The nurse often asked her older patients about their lives. She knew the elderly possess great wisdom for those willing to listen. But she had never been given such an odd answer to the question of a happy marriage.

"AREA is your secret?" the nurse asked, a bit befuddled.

"Yes. Let me explain," the gentleman said.

He began with the first letter of "AREA" and said, "The *A* stands for affection. A couple must have affection for one another, and this is greater than just attraction.

"The letter *R* stands for respect. You can have affection for someone but if you don't respect him or her, it's hard to sustain your love.

"The *E* stands for esteem, and I use it here to reflect a kind of appreciation, honor, and reverence for my spouse.

"The final *A* stands for admiration. It doesn't matter what your spouse does, whether she's a doctor, gardener, or mother. It's important that you have admiration for her." The gentleman leaned back and smiled.

The nurse was amazed that such a simple acronym could so beautifully sum up essential qualities of a long and happy marriage.

I met my wife over a decade ago when her brother-in-law introduced us. I found her immediately engaging, intelligent, articulate, and attractive.

We began dating, and as the relationship deepened, our conversations about life and love expanded. In an effort to define the things that mattered to us, our discussion inevitably turned to marriage.

"How do you define the qualities of a perfect marriage?" I asked her one night.

She smiled and said, "AREA." I was as befuddled with the answer as she was years ago, when the gentleman told her the same thing.

You see, my wife is a licensed hospice nurse. She has shepherded her own grandparents through end-of-life transitions.

I watched how she took care of her grandparents. It was with the same love, patience, and care she affords all her patients.

As the years passed, I never forgot "AREA" and the ideals behind the acronym. I strive to live up to those ideals in my marriage.

I don't know what happened to the gentleman who shared his "AREA" wisdom with my wife. I wish I could tell him how much his advice has meant to us.

Beyond the value of "AREA," there is another lesson here. Take the time to talk with the old ones among us. Slow down and listen to what they have to say.

You just might learn something that will change your life.

CHAPTER 35

THE POWER OF LETTING GO

Some things are counterintuitive. For instance, conventional wisdom tells us to never quit. Keep at it until you get it right. Author Malcolm Gladwell wrote about the now infamous ten thousand hours needed to achieve expertise in a discipline. While it's true that practice can make perfect, there are some things that we're just spinning our wheels over.

Los Angeles is full of undiscovered actors waiting tables and working in coffee shops. I'll bet many of them have been at it for a while now, acting here and there. Celebrating the bit parts they land or commercials they appear in. They don't quit, understandably, because that big break might be around the next corner. But what if it never comes?

The reality is that people quit all the time. And sometimes it's the right thing to do. In fact, quitting can sometimes be downright freeing. Some people quit an unfulfilling job. Others finally hang up those violin lessons, much to the pleasure of loved ones who endured the effort.

I quit martial arts. I got all the way to my brown belt in Danzan Rye Jujitsu. It took years. I injured my back one night and had to be carried home. Another time I was thrown so hard, it knocked my heart into supraventricular tachycardia. That led to a scary ambulance ride to an emergency room where they gave me an injection that corrected the heart rhythm. After that I did some soul searching.

I concluded that as much as I wanted to get that black belt, it wasn't worth destroying my health. I also realized that while I was a decent martial artist, I wasn't playing to my strengths. I was a much better artist than martial artist. And so I focused my efforts on painting, cartooning, and writing.

Sometimes you have to let go of people. Maybe it's a toxic relationship or a fair-weather friend. I read somewhere that we are the average of the five people we spend the most time with.

I certainly am not advocating that you abandon good friends. But sometimes we surround ourselves with people who aren't really good for us. Quitting those unhealthy relationships can be freeing, too.

David Wallace Foster once wrote, "Everything I ever let go of has claw marks on it."

We hold on to things. Sometimes it's just stuff cluttering up our life. Or painful memories in our past. Author Gordon Livingston, in his excellent book, *Too Soon Old, Too Late Smart*, wrote:

> Life can be seen as a series of relinquishments, rehearsals for the final act of letting go of our earthly selves. Why, then, is it so hard for people to surrender the past?

Livingston also wrote, "The statute of limitations has expired on most of our childhood traumas."

The power of letting go is *freedom*. It closes one door so that others may open. It can be painful but the rewards are immense.

In 2004 my father's body had enough. At eighty-three years old, having survived a heart attack and bypass surgery, he began to decline. I watched this once-brilliant administrative-law judge and former US Marine descend into the fog of dementia.

Dad was in the final throws of renal failure when I visited him in hospice. He was unconscious but the nurse said "hearing" is the last sense to go. So I held his hands. Told him everyone was fine. That I loved him.

Then I said that if he was tired to go ahead and rest. Just rest.

We got the call two hours later. He let go. I don't know what he discovered when he passed over the veil, but if my instinct about the power of letting go is true, I believe he found freedom and peace.

CHAPTER 36

A BETTER LIFE REQUIRES THIS

I have encountered a lot of broken souls in my law-enforcement career. Addicts, abusers, runaways, homeless, incarcerated, paroled, and more.

I've spoken with the haunted and angry as well as the broken and defeated. So many sad and empty eyes that once shined with hope and promise.

If there are any cracks in your protective emotional armor, this mass of tragic humanity can break your heart. So many people carrying huge emotional burdens. They're seemingly unable to break through their pain and truly live again.

There are no neat and tidy solutions that fit every injured spirit, but there is one thing we all must do if we want a better life. If you can allow yourself to do this, you will free yourself to begin living anew. You will create a path to personal growth, better habits, and greater fulfillment. What is this healing thing? *Forgive yourself.*

Father Matt Pennington is a Roman Catholic priest. He used to serve in our local church before moving on to another parish.

Father Matt has a gift for storytelling and stirring homilies. In his blog, *Journal of a Country Priest*, he touched on the notion of self-forgiveness by sharing a recording of his June 29, 2014, homily

"Rise Up!" Whether you are a person of faith or not, this message of forgiving yourself is important.

As Father Matt alluded to, perhaps you are an alcoholic who has hurt many people in your life. Maybe you chose not to have the baby and are conflicted with the decision. Or you weren't really there for your children.

Whatever it is, forgive yourself. You are not perfect; none of us are. The sins of our past don't define who we choose to be today and who we will be in the future.

Acknowledge that you stumbled. You blew it. You hurt people. Scars and bad blood and a lot of carnage may have been left in your wake.

You may have to pay some dues; make things as right as you can; apologize to those hurt. Some will never forgive you.

But in the end, you have to forgive yourself. You have to unshackle that burden. Allow for the statute of limitations on past transgressions to end.

I know, you don't think you deserve it. You don't think you can. But you're wrong.

It really is possible to forgive yourself. And then move on. Why? Because a better life requires this.

CHAPTER 37

YOUR SECOND DEATH AND HOW TO TRANSCEND IT

Ted Strollo was an Italian immigrant and master woodcarver who came to California for a better life. He had few possessions, no family, and no job.

He built a little cabin in the woods above Los Gatos. He drank acorn coffee. He was a kind man and a master woodworker. Out of a single piece of wood, he created an amazing sculpture with perfect cylindrical balls in the middle. He called the piece his "mystery tree of life."

Ted Strollo's life was a quiet and solitary one, until the day he was struck by a vehicle and hurled twenty feet through the air.

The mystery tree of life
My father, an administrative-law judge, was on his way home from work when he witnessed the accident. He pulled over and rendered aid as best he could. He followed the ambulance to the hospital and spoke to the police and doctors.

My father learned that the victim was an Italian immigrant named Ted Strollo and that he had no family. He discovered that

Ted had no money for legal representation, so he decided to intervene and help.

Ted spent over a month at our home recuperating. He stayed in our guest room, and my mother prepared his meals and did his laundry. When he recovered my father found him an affordable apartment and secured some state benefits.

We used to visit Ted on weekends. My father would buy him Stella Dora cookies and new socks. Dad once told me, "Johnny, the elderly are often forgotten and overlooked. They have much to teach us, if we're willing to take the time and listen." I never forgot that.

Before Ted Strollo passed away, he gave my father his prized wooden sculpture, the "mystery tree of life." We kept it in our family for many years before Dad donated it to an Italian cultural society.

The son became the father

My father lost his battle with dementia and renal complications in 2004. It had been a difficult couple of years for me. In many ways, the father became the son, and the son became the father. I was so thankful I had the opportunity to be there for him.

I shepherded my father through his medical odyssey and handled all the legal arrangements for my mother. We held a beautiful memorial, buried Dad, and tried to return to our daily lives.

I read once about something called "the second death." When we die, our loved ones live on and remember us. They reminisce about the past and our lives together. They look at the old photographs.

Sometimes they pass down stories about us to their grandchildren. But eventually, we are forgotten. And that is our "second death."

The superpower in us all

Each of us holds a superpower within us. Not the kind of superpower we see in Spiderman movies. It's a real superpower that can be wielded by young and old alike.

I watched my father use his superpower the day he helped Ted Strollo and brought him home to recuperate. My mother used her superpower too, cooking and caring for Ted.

What is this mysterious superpower? *Kindness* toward others.

Each of us has the power to improve the lives of others. Whether serving the hungry in a soup kitchen, nursing an Italian immigrant back to health, or helping your kids with their homework.

Perhaps we will never know how our charitable actions help redirect a wayward soul. Maybe our kindnesses will be forgotten with subsequent generations as we approach our "second death."

That's okay. True heroes don't act for personal glory but for the greater good.

Who knows how many acts of kindness my father set in motion by helping Ted Strollo? How many people did Ted Strollo positively touch in his remaining years?

A sort of grace in this world

We may never know, but kindness and charitable actions toward others produce a sort of grace in this world. Such actions make the world a better place. They elevate humanity.

We may forget the names of these angels on earth who selflessly help others, but through their kindnesses and charity, they make a difference.

When we emulate them, we inch a bit closer to the divine. And that is a much greater thing than personal legacy.

Learn to wield your superpower. Your act of kindness today may help someone assist another tomorrow. A positive chain reaction will bloom, thus improving the lives of many down through the generations.

People who spread kindness and charity among others may never see the positive ripples, but they contribute to the best of us.

In this way we transcend our "second death" and become part of the eternal dignity of mankind.

CHAPTER 38

THE MOST IMPORTANT QUALITY TO LOOK FOR IN A SIGNIFICANT OTHER

One of the benefits of a career in law enforcement is that your eyes are opened to the many failures of humanity. You encounter despair, loss, anguish, addictions, and broken lives.

It's not fun to see this stuff, but it can teach you a lot about what to avoid in your own life. To that end, I'd like to share with you a bit of advice about dating and relationships.

I don't proclaim to be any kind of expert, but I've seen my share of dysfunctional relationships. Responding to countless domestic fights over the years gave me some insight. Particularly, I discovered the single most important quality to look for in a significant other. That quality is *kindness.*

Most guys I know tend to focus on looks first. And that's where they get into trouble. Don't get me wrong, you definitely want to be attracted to the person you're dating but not at the expense of more important qualities.

One of my favorite analogies is this: Dating is a lot like buying a car. You can have that Italian Ferrari if you want to, but the maintenance costs are gonna kill you!

Some women I've known focused on money. This one is a slippery slope as well. Money is nice but doesn't guarantee a happy relationship. Shared interests can increase compatibility, but at the end of the day, kindness is the most important quality.

Look for how your date treats other people. Does she thank the water boy at a restaurant? Is he an impatient driver, cutting people off and yelling? How does she treat her parents? Does he tend to speak well of others or gossip and always see the worst in people?

I can't think of a single domestic violence case I ever handled that was started by a kind person. Obviously, even kind people can have their shortcomings. A person could be kind and still be a slob, for example. For that reason, kindness alone doesn't seal the deal. But more often than not, a kind person will bring you a much more pleasant life than an angry or moody person.

Be aware that people always try to put their best foot forward when meeting others. Some potential suitors may appear kind at first, but give it some time.

A person's past history is hard to hide for long, and his/her true stripes usually manifest before long. The world is full of so many angry, maladjusted, entitled, shallow, and opportunistic people. But it's also full of some wonderful, emotionally mature, kind souls.

If you are single and searching for that perfect someone, make sure you put kindness at the top of your "must-have" qualities in a significant other. Doing so just might spare you a lot of pain, heartache, and unhappiness.

CHAPTER 39
WHY THE THREE BS CAN RUIN YOUR LIFE

Back in my police academy days, we had many fine instructors who taught us how to become police officers, but the advice and wisdom of one instructor never left me.

He was a grizzled old sergeant who came in to teach us about the penal code. He had a photographic memory and could recall minute details of the many laws we would be sworn to enforce.

He taught us a lot, but his personal reflections about the foibles of man were perhaps his most memorable lessons. The standout was a brief lecture on the dangers of the "three Bs."

"Booze, Babes, and Bucks," said the old sergeant, "have been the downfall of too many cops, not to mention politicians, movie stars, and society!" The good sergeant launched into a cautionary sermon with many colorful examples, but let me summarize the core points.

"Booze" obviously refers to alcohol and other drugs. Many a good cop has injured or lost his/her career over alcohol or drugs. Alcohol fuels poor decision making that leads to things like drunk driving, domestic upsets, and sick days.

There's nothing wrong with the occasional beer bust or end-of-shift choir practice, but for some this becomes a slippery slope into a regular lifestyle choice.

"Babes" refers to just that, all the physically attractive people you meet. It's normal to appreciate the good looks of another, but some people fall prey to their carnal appetite.

We have all met the skirt chasers and flirts who ruin their marriages, reputations, and lives over infidelity. Even pornography fits under the "Babes" warning because of the pain it can bring to relationships and erosion of your character.

"Bucks" is all about the travails of money management. Instant gratification is always battling with our personal discipline. We've all known people who are mortgaged to the hilt and maxed out with their credit cards, but somehow they still go on vacation and eat out.

I've seen cops over the years take second jobs to make ends meet, but they're exhausted at work and burned out. And we all know the gal who loves to try her luck at the card tables or buys lottery tickets weekly. Poor money management and credit debt have ruined many lives.

I never forgot the "three Bs," and hope that the old sergeant's life lesson might help you stay focused on your own path.

Drink in moderation or not at all if you have no talent for it. Stay loyal to your relationship or exit honorably. Finally, live within your means, and sacrifice when necessary to avoid debt.

Avoid the "three Bs," and you'll save yourself a lot of grief and heartache.

CHAPTER 40

WHAT MICHELANGELO CAN TEACH US ABOUT SUCCESS

Have you ever been given a job assignment you really didn't want to do? If so, then you have something in common with Michelangelo, the famous Renaissance sculptor, painter, architect, and poet.

Apart from Leonardo da Vinci, Michelangelo is arguably the greatest artist of all time. He may have been prodigious, brilliant, and divinely inspired, but that doesn't mean he wasn't human. And mere humans can be cranky.

Most people are familiar with the Sistine Chapel in Vatican City, Rome. Aside from serving as a venue for the election of new popes via a conclave of the College of Cardinals, the Sistine Chapel is most notable for its remarkable fresco paintings. Most famous of all are the frescoes by Michelangelo.

Pope Julius II commissioned Michelangelo to paint the Sistine Chapel, but Michelangelo considered himself a sculptor. In fact, he was busy with a sculpting project when the good pope came knocking with the Sistine Chapel job. He didn't want to take the commission. He actually looked down on painting. He was a sculptor, for crying out loud! But what's a poor Renaissance superstar to do, say no to the pope?

Michelangelo had to construct special scaffolds to paint the Sistine Chapel. And despite conventional wisdom, he didn't actually lie down on the scaffolds to paint. He stood up. He labored on the project from 1508 until 1512.

Johann Wolfgang von Goethe, the German writer and statesman, said this about Michelangelo's Sistine Chapel: "Without having seen the Sistine Chapel one can form no appreciable idea of what one man is capable of achieving."

Few if any among us possess the monumental artistic talent of Michelangelo. But beyond his artistic skill, Michelangelo does demonstrate another skill that is within our grasp. What Michelangelo can teach us about success is simply this: you have to show up.

Yes, talent and skill matter. But the world is full of talented, skilled individuals who fail. The reason why is that they are unable to consistently show up. It's our human inclination to grow bored with routine and repetition. We start new projects and goals with great gusto. But after a bit, we fizzle out.

What often separates the successful from the unsuccessful is consistency. Michelangelo wanted to sculpt, but nevertheless he spent over four years painting instead. He showed up. Day in and day out. Straddling awkward scaffolds, painting masterful frescoes that the world still marvels at.

Certainly there were days he loathed the effort. In fact, he wrote to friends about the strain of his labors. But he kept showing up. If you want to lose weight, you'll need to follow Michelangelo's example. You'll have to stick to that diet and exercise.

If you want to quit the liquor for good, you'll have to overcome those cravings. One day at a time. If you want to succeed as an entrepreneur, you'll have to keep swinging the bat every day. Weather the ups and downs. Day after day.

In all these things, you have to show up. Again and again. Because that's what separates the ones who succeed from the ones who don't. And that's what Michelangelo can teach us about success.

CHAPTER 41

LESSONS ON LOVE AND DEATH FROM AN OAK TREE

The city leaders determined, reluctantly, that the old man had to come down. He stood feebly in the middle of a city park. But he was dying now. The children who played beneath his protective canopy were at risk. Large, brittle branches could fall.

Some of his twisted and gnarled limbs were held up by huge wooden posts. Crutches for an old yet dignified man. A man full of stories. A man who provided home and sanctuary to squirrels, woodpeckers, and other creatures. Shade for children.

For twenty-five years I passed the old gentleman as he stood sentry in the park, adjacent to city hall and the police department where I work. How many generations has he overseen? How many children played among his fallen acorns and bark?

The arborist's report was clear. He was dying and likely to fall down before long. And so phone calls were made and workers arrived. With saws and shears, the old man was dismantled. Whittled away until, in a final salute, his trunk was felled, and it was all over.

Days later I saw a lone squirrel at the edge of the grass. He was spying the stump, the only remaining vestige of the old man's grandeur. It looked like the squirrel was paying his respects.

The park is more open now. Sunshine freely illuminates the open lawn where kids have more space for football. Younger oak trees can be seen more clearly. Aspirants, perhaps, to someday become as proud and tall as the old man.

Our lives are similar to oak trees. Much like acorns, we come from humble origins. We too grow up among the sunshine, rain, and fresh air. Our skin ages as bark gnarls. Like the hidden, concentric rings inside the tree trunk, our minds build layers of memories and knowledge. Sometimes we need crutches, too. Sometimes surgeons.

And when we stand no more, our lives are marked with tombstones. Just as the fallen oak's life is marked by the remaining stump.

What are we to learn about life from an old oak tree? Maybe that we should strive to stand tall. Refuse to bend when life's challenges and indignities are foisted upon us.

Perhaps we should extend our arms as loving branches for all who come into our meadow. Shed a few tears as the oak shed a few acorns. Breathe deeply like the tree canopy absorbs the breeze. Provide shelter for our family.

And when the younger oaks come into their own, we should bow out gracefully. Exit the meadow knowing that we did our best, spread some love, and shared some laughter.

Before the old stump was ground down and completely gone, I saw some children playing on it. I thought how sad that they won't get to enjoy the old oak like I did.

The long shadow of the old oak may be gone but not the memory of him.

CHAPTER 42

WHY YOU NEED TO CLIMB THAT MOUNTAIN

This is going to be short and to the point. I want you to climb that mountain. One step at a time. Climb that mountain.

I know you've got some good excuses. Work steals a lot of time. There's that daily commute. The mortgage is like a monthly ball and chain. It slows you down, but you need the house. You need the job. After all, it provides the health care and some dental coverage. I get it.

You're sick of all the blogging gurus lecturing about how to live our lives. And then there's Facebook. So many people documenting their glamorous lives. Ski trips, rock concerts, parties, cool pictures, fit bodies, and smiles. Makes you feel like your own life is a dull version of ground hog day.

Who has time for all those elegant photos and snappy memes about extraordinary living? Doesn't anyone have a demanding job, commitments, deadlines, and fatigue?

Somehow, beyond the nine-to-five routine, day care runs, and obligations, you have to squeeze in your art. You know, that sad little studio in the closet. Or maybe the garage.

Ah, the garage. That was my first studio. It was chilly. In the summer it was warm. So I'd open the garage door and uninvited condo neighbors would stroll in to render judgment.

"Is that Yosemite you're painting?" one neighbor would ask.

"Nope. Idaho. Thanks. Think I'll scrape it and call it a day." Okay, I didn't really say that, but you get the gist. Sometimes you want to paint and be left alone.

My dear fellow artist, keep climbing that mountain. Don't give up on your creative spirit. Carve out time where you can. Don't let the digital lives of others depress you. Beyond the pretty pictures and smiles, they have their struggles too.

Your art is like a dear old friend. She's always there. Always happy to see you when you can visit.

They say during our parenting years that the days are long but the years are short. It's true. The diapers, sleepless nights, little league, messy rooms, and teenage angst. It'll pass and you'll wonder where it went. When you're in the thick of it that sounds far away. It isn't. But even during those hectic years, there is time for art. "Where? How?" you might ask.

Start by giving the television a vacation. Same with that enticing laptop, with its digital rabbit holes. A quick jaunt through your Facebook timeline can kill an hour or more. That could be time in the studio.

Yes, you're tired. The creative mood is distant or asleep. Pick up the brush anyway. Push some paint around. Craft some poetry in that Moleskine journal. See what you can shape with that clay. What musical arrangement you can craft?

Half the battle is just showing up. It works even better if you can set a schedule. Every morning at 5:30 a.m. Or an hour before bed. Your internal rhythms will dictate.

You need to climb that mountain. Being an artist requires fortitude. You have to be a persistent soul. You'll have to learn how to say no to people. In a nice way, of course. But people will always spend your time for you, if you let them.

I quit a service club I had been in for years. Lots of great people in that club. But my full-time work as a police chief and family commitments left little margin for writing and painting. And I need that. Art rebalances me.

Seek simplicity whenever you can. I've learned that less is more. I used to run a personal writing blog on a WordPress platform. It was versatile but the updates, plug-ins, and other technical difficulties were a pain.

So I moved it to an elegant template platform. Guess what? Life is so much easier. Everything is handled. No more updates and digital subscriber attacks. It just works. My traffic improved. Now all I have to do is focus on creating. Nice and simple.

Do me a favor. If you're discouraged or tired, don't give up. Keep climbing that mountain. Don't worry about those artists who are further along than you. This is your journey, not theirs.

Push yourself; forgive yourself, but keep climbing that mountain. There is great joy in art and creativity, no matter what particular point you are on the mountain. Besides, it's a beautiful mountain. The view is great, and it's a joyous place to spend your time.

CHAPTER 43

HOW TO TAKE CHARGE OF YOUR UNHAPPINESS

When my son was little, I often took him to the local playground to burn off some steam. I was a young cop back then, frequently assigned to graveyard shifts. The playground visits were great because my son got to play with other kids and I could read my newspaper and relax. Except for one thing. The constant "Hey, Dad, look at me!"

Kids thrive on attention. Even on the playground with tons of other pip-squeaks, our children want an audience. They want to know we're watching. They want our interest and approval. Which is fine, because we're dealing with young spirits and developing personalities. Our interest, affection, and reassurance show our kids we love them.

Unhappy campers at work
When I became a supervisor at work, I discovered how important it was to take an interest in my subordinates. I'd craft employee-of-the-month awards, point out exemplary work, and try to be encouraging.

Invariably, there were always a few unhappy campers. Employees who always had a complaint, blamed management for all their woes, and infected others with their negativity.

Conversely, there were also a small number of employees who never complained. They seemed to go through their workdays blissfully. While they appreciated recognition, it wasn't as important to them.

The same phenomena can be found in relationships. Some people are well adjusted and secure in their relationships, while others persistently complain. As a cop I've been to countless domestic squabbles. Predominantly, the arguments were because one person was not doing something for the other.

Don't be held hostage by others
Bottom line, there are a lot of unhappy people out there. And the reason a lot of them are unhappy? Because they constantly seek the approval of others. Relying on others for validation is a recipe for failure. If you want to take charge of your unhappiness, stop relying on the approval and attention of others. Chart your own course, and do what fulfills you.

It's fine when you're six years old and you want Dad to see how well you ride your bike. But you're an adult now. "Happiness comes from within" is more than a cliché. It happens to be largely true.

If you look to your spouse or boss to validate your life, you're going to be disappointed. It's not their job. Your spouse should complement your life, not be responsible for it. And your boss should be like a coach, not a therapist.

Author and psychologist Gordon Livingston wrote, "Any relationship is under the control of the person who cares the least." If you hinge your happiness on your spouse's approval and attention, then you empower him/her over you. That's crazy.

Seeking honest feedback and input is one thing. We should all allow for constructive criticism. But the minute we put our emotional well-being on the mercy of others, we're on thin ice.

Accept feedback, but don't be ruled by it

Yes, we need love and support in our lives. Yes, it's gratifying to be celebrated and recognized for our work and contributions. But you've got to do things mainly because it's gratifying to you alone.

Do work that pleases you and the rest will take care of itself. This doesn't mean being selfish. We should always be considerate of coworkers and our spouses. Sometimes we need to sacrifice things for others. But you must do things that satisfy your own soul, not the whims of others.

Pursue your passions. Find work that's meaningful to you. Take responsibility for your own happiness. Be self-determined. Don't export your happiness to the opinions of others.

You're no longer six years old on the playground. Stop relying on the approval and validation of others. The answer to your happiness lies within yourself. It always has.

CHAPTER 44

THREE REASONS WHY ELEGANCE IS BETTER THAN WINNING

Several years ago my wife whisked me away for my birthday to Anderson Valley, located near the coastal region of Mendocino County in Northern California. Our lodging was the Philo Pottery Inn, a charming little bed and breakfast that since closed down. Beyond the beautiful scenery, the primary purpose of our weekend was to attend a wonderful Alsace wine dinner at Scharffenberger Cellars.

We dressed up for the event and were seated at a large table full of friendly strangers. As the evening unfolded, appetizers and tasty dishes were paired with outstanding wine selections. Then, at some point in the dinner conversation, a woman inexplicably ventured into politics. She proclaimed her low opinion of the president of the United States. Others at the table nodded in agreement. Except for me.

Spoiling for a fight
I grew up in a household of readers. My father, an administrative-law judge and learned man, often held court at dinnertime. We'd discuss current events, news, and politics. I couldn't compete with

my father's expansive knowledge of history, but I enjoyed jousting with him on political issues.

I grew to enjoy lively debate; however, I learned that it's generally bad form to make partisan political comments to a table full of strangers. It's just presumptuous and a little arrogant to drop political bombs among polite company. So, when that woman was finished dissing the president, I challenged her. "I don't think I could disagree with you more."

Well. Things got interesting. Real fast. The woman was a Berkeley attorney. I was a cocky law-enforcement professional with a graduate degree. Before the dessert and aged port arrived, the woman and I were engaged in a heated debate.

The fool chatters while the wise man listens
My wife rolled her eyes and slid across the table to converse with a quiet woman who seemed unimpressed with the political banter. But the most fascinating chap at the table was an elegant Irish gentleman. He had white hair and was impeccably dressed and nonplussed by the political salvos being hurled back and forth. The gentleman's name was Guinness McFadden.

My wife, who has far more common sense than me, stayed completely out of the political morass. Apparently others got tired of it as well, and the table thinned. Mr. McFadden was queried at one point to offer an opinion.

I recall that he raised an eyebrow and briefly shared a bit of his military background. Somehow he managed to deliver a salient yet nonpartisan point. And with that he fell silent again. Content to let us exhaust ourselves.

Later that night, back at the Philo Pottery Inn, I sensed my wife's displeasure. "That woman should know better. You can't drop political bombs and expect everyone to agree with you," I reasoned.

An Artful Life

My wife countered with her observations of Guinness McFadden. About how dignified he was. Above the fray. Clearly capable of delivering trenchant, probably devastating insights that would have ended the debate. But he didn't. Too much of a gentleman.

Mistakes of youth
I was younger then. It took less to tease an argument out of me. I didn't understand that such debates were often of little consequence. People believe what they believe.

Mr. McFadden obviously knew this. He had wisdom and much more life experience on his side. In fact, he's quite a remarkable guy. He turned down an Ivy League scholarship to attend the University of Norte Dame. He earned a bronze star in Vietnam. In Potter Valley, where he makes wine, he is also a pioneer in the Mendocino organic movement.

As the years marched on, I often thought about our little weekend getaway to Mendocino County. Over time, I learned to stand down when someone tossed out a provocative remark or political statement. I took a page from Guinness McFadden, with my wife's approval. I guess wisdom, like caviar, is an acquired taste. You need some experience and time to develop it.

Wolves and monkeys
People often say that man's natural inclination is toward violence and war. I remember a quote by the historians Will and Ariel Durant: "No one ever wants to recognize the inexorable periodicity of war." Perhaps they're right. In many ways men can be like wolves. They like to pack together, go on the hunt, and fight. They respect strength and usually pick a leader of the pack.

But men can also be like monkeys. They can form tight bonds, families, and supportive networks. They can look out for one another and demonstrate great tenderness.

I'd like to think that man's deeper instinct bends toward elegance, peacefulness, and love. Maybe that's why aged felons who get out of prison infrequently reoffend. They're older and hopefully wiser. All the piss and vinegar of youth is spent, and the mind turns to more important concerns. Thoughts about purpose. Legacy.

Choose elegance over winning
If you want to please your wife, impress fellow dinner guests, and actually enjoy your dessert, here's some advice for you. Namely, three reasons why elegance is better than winning.

1. You won't look and sound like a jerk. You might have all the answers and even be right, but sometimes you lose even when you win an argument.
2. Winning rarely changes people's minds. As noted above, people believe what they believe. Try convincing a Palestinian that Israel should exist. Or vice versa. Same thing with apologists and atheists. People become entrenched in their beliefs. Beating someone in a debate may feel good; but have you really influenced your opponent?
3. Elegance transcends biases. It didn't really matter to me what side of the political fence Guinness McFadden was on. I was far more intrigued and impressed with his kind demeanor, distinguished flair, and friendly disposition. Not to mention the fact that my wife was more smitten with how he behaved at dinner than me.

I have nothing against wolves, but they do help illustrate my point. The next time you are tempted to jump into the fray, snarl your fangs, and nip at the heels of your political opponent, take pause.

An Artful Life

Picture those amazing gorillas we see in nature films, sitting placidly in a lush rain forest, rocking their babies, and grooming one another. Which better illustrates what we should strive for?

Guinness McFadden already figured this all out. Thanks to his example, my wife's gentle reinforcement, and the mellowing refinement of time, I'm starting to figure it out too. Elegance is better than winning.

CHAPTER 45

HOW TO LIVE A BETTER LIFE IN THREE KEYS

Irma Hincenbergs and her husband had a nice life in Latvia. She was an accomplished piano teacher and he a banker. But everything changed when Latvia became occupied by the Soviet Union from 1944 to 1991.

Under the Soviet occupation, thousands of Latvians were sent to Siberian camps, killed, or forced into exile. According to Wikipedia, many Latvians fled in fishermen's boats and ships to Sweden and Germany, from where until 1951, they drifted to various parts of the Western world (mostly Australia and North America). Approximately 150,000 Latvians ended up in exile in the West. Irma and her husband were among those exiles, eventually landing in Los Gatos, California. My hometown.

Over the years they managed to craft a new life. Irma began teaching piano again, and her husband found work. They settled into a quaint Victorian house in downtown Los Gatos. This was before the emergence of Silicon Valley, when home prices were still within reach.

Around this time, my father had invested in a baby grand piano that my mother enjoyed plinking on. Before long, she decided that piano lessons were in order. One way or another, she discovered Irma Hincenbergs and began taking lessons.

My mother's nightly piano playing sparked my own curiosity about music. Soon I was experimenting on the piano. I had a good ear for music and a natural facility on the keyboard. It didn't take long before my mother drove me down to meet Mrs. Hincenbergs. That led to several years of weekly lessons every Friday after school.

Mrs. Hincenbergs was a disciplined but kindly woman. She shepherded me through my scales, sheet music, and repetitive exercises. She would often blurt out, "No, no, no…" in the middle of a piece. She'd grab my fingers and reposition them. She'd look me in the eye, explaining the mood or intent of the music. It was often over my head, but I nodded in agreement and began anew.

She had the softest hands I'd ever felt. Her voice was soothing and tranquil. Tried as I did to focus on the music, her gentle comments and hand repositioning often made me feel sleepy. But I did learn and eventually was able to play works like Claude Debussy's "Clair de Lune."

Irma Hincenbergs taught me three keys to better music and a better life:

1. Practice makes perfect.
2. Consistency is key.
3. Have a soft touch.

I learned the absolute value of practice. Proficiency and high art cannot be achieved without long and disciplined practice. There just aren't any shortcuts to excellence.

It soon became apparent that consistency was the companion of practice. Inconsistent practice slows one's progress. Only with consistency can practice produce real progress. And Irma Hincenbergs always knew when I fell short with either.

During my time with Mrs. Hincenbergs, I discovered rock music, much to her chagrin. As a result, I became a bit too exuberant on the keyboard. This invited a series of lectures about the ugly sound of "pounding" on the keyboard.

I was told that it was far more eloquent and refined to develop a soft touch. Less, I learned, was often more. Such that when an expressive note was called for, it held so much more impact and feeling.

I was too immature and unsophisticated back then to understand the broader context of Mrs. Hincenbergs's teachings. Which is too bad. Because she passed on before I ever really got it. Before I realized that practice, consistency, and a soft touch have value beyond playing the piano. They are key attributes to a better life.

Irma Hincenbergs was an elderly Latvian immigrant, whose entire life was uprooted by the Soviet invasion of her country. She had a right to be angry and surely did voice her hatred of the Soviet Union at times. But her love of music never faltered, nor her knack for shaping young pianists.

Beyond the scales and keyboard exercises, my weekly lessons and consistent practice instilled some important disciplines in me. And I learned to have a soft touch not only on the piano but in life too. My piano playing taught me other things, like rhythm and cadence. Qualities that inform my writing and creative efforts.

I never got to say good-bye to Irma Hincenbergs. I went off to college, and somewhere in those years, she passed on. But her life lessons still manifest in my habits today. Her soft hands, Latvian accent, and affectionate presence live on in my memory.

Thank you, Irma Hincenbergs. May your heavenly piano serenade the angels through eternity.

CHAPTER 46

I FOUND MY WAY ON THE DAY THEY STOPPED MY HEART

The emergency room doctor looked squarely into my eyes. She was calm and focused. I spied the syringe in her right hand. Next to her was a nurse. The nurse was holding a syringe of her own. "This can't be good," I thought.

"John, I'm going to give you an injection, and you might feel a slight flutter in your chest. Try to relax." The doctor meant to reassure me. I tried to relax. No luck.

There was an IV slipped into the antecubital area of my arm. That's the part of your arm that folds inward, opposite the elbow. The doctor then attached the syringe to the IV, delivering the medicine. No pain, but I definitely felt the "flutter" in my chest. At the time, I didn't understand what was happening. Which was good. Because the doctor just stopped my heart.

The jujitsu injury
Before the ambulance arrived and rushed me off to the ER, I was participating in a martial arts demonstration. The instructor selected me for the demo because I was a brown belt, which is just below black belt. Sounds impressive, but mostly it meant that I

was the "attacker." The "attacker" is the one the instructor gets to throw around like a rag doll.

The jujitsu I trained in was a hard style. Lots of grappling, throws, flips, and such. Somewhere in the middle of the demo, the instructor performed a dynamic throw. Down I went, into what I thought was a beautifully executed fall. But when I got up, something was wrong.

I felt these consistent palpitations in my chest. Nothing like a heart attack but alarming nonetheless. One of my fellow students was a doctor and immediately read my behavior. "You okay?" he asked. I told him what I was experiencing. He had me sit down and tried a few tricks, to no avail. Then he said, "I think you're having SVT. We should run you over to the hospital to straighten that out."

Calm before the storm
Don't you just love doctors? So calm. So unflappable. I'm in the throes of SVT (supraventricular tachycardia) and my doctor buddy suggests I pop over to the ER. Get things "straightened" out. Like I'm going to a hair appointment! But I have to admit, his calm reassurance kept me from panicking.

Someone called the ambulance, and the EMTs arrived in short order. I was seated on the dojo floor with the entire class standing around me. Not the way to attract a crowd. The EMTs foisted me onto a gurney and set about their work. Checking vitals, chattering in medical terms.

In hindsight, I shouldn't have been surprised. I was a police sergeant back then and had just come off a graveyard shift. With no sleep and two coffees under my belt, I rolled into morning class. I should have been in bed. But I'd grown accustomed to sacrificing sleep to reach my goals.

Clearly, I was exhausted and running on empty. That reality, combined with the perfect throw to the mat, jarred my heart. The injury was a fluke, really. The emergency room nurse would later tell me about a thirty-five-year-old mother they treated the week before. She was wrestling with her young son when he kicked her in the chest. An innocent little kick during horseplay. But that's all it took, and the mother landed in the ER with SVT.

The miracle of modern medicine
The injection the doctor gave me effectively stops your heart. But only for a millisecond. The injection causes your heart to return to a normal sinus rhythm. Fortunately for me, it worked like a charm. Which was good. Because the nurse with the other syringe was standing by with medicine to start my heart (in case it didn't correct on its own.) I also learned that sometimes they have to transition to electric shocks.

Once the old ticker was behaving again, the ER doctor and staff said I could sign some papers and head home. I was still freaked out by the whole incident. I would later schedule appointments with my primary care physician, obtain all the ER records, and so on. My doctor had me wear a heart monitor for twenty-four hours. He ran some tests. Long story short, I was fit as a fiddle.

Introspection and new directions
The whole affair led to some serious introspection. I began to ask myself questions about why I was studying martial arts. What were my goals? My direction? Was I happy?

I resumed my martial arts training after the incident, but (pardon the pun) my heart was no longer in it. I realized that my true talent and calling involved the creative arts. Painting, cartooning, and writing.

I enjoyed training in jujitsu and was close to my black belt. But I knew I would only be an adequate martial artist. Why was I spinning my wheels in the dojo when I should be painting, writing, and refining my creative potential?

So I quit. It wasn't easy. As a cop, I was trained to "never give up." But sometimes we need to pivot. We need to look deep inside ourselves and figure out what our calling is. Quitting, when done thoughtfully, can free us to pursue what we were meant to do.

I envy my friends who went on to achieve their black belts. It's an accomplishment to be proud of. But I'm equally proud of my artistic growth. Jujitsu training brought me moments of joy, interspersed with periods of pain, frustration, and fear.

When I paint and write, time stands still. I am completely immersed. Lost in the moment. My creative efforts bring me great joy. As scary as that day in the ER was, it was the day I found my way. The day I recognized that I was on the wrong path.

I don't recommend suffering a SVT to clarify your true calling, but that's how it happened for me. And it has made all the difference.

CHAPTER 47

HOW TO AVOID DROWNING IN THE DEEP END OF LIFE

Ever dive into the deep end of a pool? The further down you go, the more pressure you feel. It's from the weight of all that water above you. Descend to the bottom of the shallow end and there's much less weight. If you think about it, swimming under water is the perfect metaphor for life.

When we are young, we tip our toes in the water. We cautiously try new things, usually under the protective watch of our parents. They act as our lifeguards. With confidence and a few years under our belt, we learn to tread water and swim. We discover how to risk a bit. We hold our breath and venture underwater. Not unlike the experience of attending a new school. Or giving our first class presentation.

With life experience and some maturity, we begin to swim further from the shallow end. The lifeguards still eye us but with a bit less trepidation. We feel the freedom of swimming further and deeper. Much like going off to college. Or starting that first big job.

When I was a kid, I had a buddy whose parents belonged to a private swim club. I was often invited during the summer months to come with them to the swim club. Kids were required to pass a swim test before they were allowed to venture into the deep end or use the diving board. My buddy was braver than me. He took the test, passed, and soon was waving to me from the diving board. It took me months. But one day, I went for it.

Passing that swim test was a lot like earning a diploma from high school or college. It opened a door for me. I was now allowed to swim in the deep waters. Like an adult.

Over time, swimming in the deep end becomes routine. It loses its specialness. Like a career you worked hard to grow in, sometimes you reach a level of ambivalence. Maybe even boredom. And that's when it can get dangerous. When you run the risk of drowning.

The accumulation of years is a lot like the weight of water above you in the deep end. We shoulder few burdens as children. Swimming to the bottom of the shallow end is easier. Less weight above us. Less responsibilities and worries. But swimming through the currents of the deep end is different. There's a lot of weight above us. The weight of regrets. Aging. Health challenges. Divorce. Loss.

The celebrated American novelist David Wallace Foster clearly swam in the deep end of life. Educated at Amherst College, he majored in English and philosophy. His philosophy senior thesis was in modal logic. He was a deep-thinking guy. But as writer Alexander Nazaryan wrote in *Newsweek* magazine, he was a "turbulent genius." He struggled mightily with depression. Yet in one commencement speech, he warned against disillusionment, urging us to embrace compassion, mindfulness, and existentialism.

David Wallace Foster navigated the currents far below the surface of the deep end. But his exquisite mind was unable to reconcile the pain. The weight of all that water. And so, at forty-six years old, he hung himself. He drowned in the deep end of life.

I have already explored the difficult subject of suicide in a past article. This article is about adulthood, the weight of responsibilities, and how to survive the deep end of life.

You see, we're all consigned to a certain degree of routine, commitments, and difficulties. Alexander Nazaryan's *Newsweek* article mentioned the Soviet-born poet Joseph Brodsky, who said to a graduating Dartmouth class that "a substantial part of what lies ahead of you is going to be claimed by boredom."

Much of life contains amazing moments, like marriage and children and career milestones. But a great deal of life also contains mundane routine. Commutes. Meetings. Obligations. Boredom. These things reflect the weight of water above you in the deep end.

If we are to surface safely from the deep waters of life, we must rely on certain buoys. They are lifelines. They literally lift us up. The three most important buoys are as follows:

1. **Health.** Take care of yourself. You can't last long in the water if you're unhealthy. And you'll be no good to other swimmers in distress.
2. **Family.** Who will be there to hand you a towel when you emerge from cold waters? Who will swim with you? Family are the buoys in life that help keep us afloat.
3. **Passion.** You need something beyond family that you love. That you really care about. If you don't have that, then the will to work your way back to the surface may wane. Don't let boredom, routine, and regrets weigh you down. Passion (for your art, your cause, your charity or faith) is what will help you stay afloat.

There will be hot days ahead. Times when you'll want to cool off and refresh. So dive into that pool of life and swim. Venture into the deep end when you're ready. But equip yourself. Be smart about it. Remember the important buoys of health, family, and passion. Do that, and you'll avoid drowning in the deep end of life. Instead, you'll have braved the deep waters and emerged. Refreshed, invigorated, and alive.

CHAPTER 48

EMBRACE CONSTRUCTIVE CRITICISM FOR A BETTER YOU

I pay a guy who's a professional writer to read my stuff and shred it. The way it works is I slave over an article and pour out my best creative effort. I harness disparate thoughts and the collision of ideas into solid literary prose. Something sure to move readers deeply. Maybe even lead to a book deal.

When I finish my articles, I sit back with a grin. "This one's the bomb," I'll think to myself. But before I hit the publish button, I send the piece over to my writing coach. "Just to tie up any loose ends," I tell myself.

But who am I kidding? Before long, my tattered piece of literary brilliance lands back in my in-box. All marked up. Little arrows attached to succinct comments. "You started off okay, but it fell apart here," one comment might say. "What I think you meant to say is this…" another notation reads. "Well, at least you can still draw cartoons." Okay, my coach didn't actually write that one, but you get the point.

Your mom will always be your biggest fan. Same with your close friends. All artistic souls need support from time to time. But if you're serious about becoming a better you, you need objectivity. A critical eye. Whether it's a brutally honest writing coach or merciless personal trainer, you have to embrace constructive criticism.

Think back in school to the tough teachers you had. Not the ones who handed out easy A's but the ones that made you work your butt off for that B. You felt a greater sense of accomplishment with the tough teachers. Because you knew you really earned that grade.

Same thing with becoming a better you. If you're serious about improving your fitness or art or craft, you need to find out what's not working. What's broken or flawed. To do that you need a tough teacher. An impartial, lesser honest critic. Someone who won't pull any punches. It won't be easy, but you'll adjust. So long as the coach or instructor you use is qualified, constructive, and honest, you'll benefit from his/her counsel.

I often hear about today's helicopter parents, teachers, and coaches who protect young self-esteems and make sure everyone gets a trophy. Well intentioned, I'm sure. I was a somewhat protective parent myself. But excessive praise sets kids up later in life for a difficult reality check. When they find out the truth. When the real world crashes down on them. When they discover that there are others who perform better.

If you're a parent, don't be afraid to challenge your kids with constructive criticism. Be kind but honest. My dad was like that. He wasn't afraid to give it to me straight. If he saw flaws in my artwork, he'd point them out. But on the occasions he praised my work, it meant so much more to me.

I didn't send this article to my writing coach, so no doubt it could use some polish. But hopefully you get the point. Embrace constructive criticism if you're serious about becoming a better you. It might mean paying someone to be honest, but consider it money well spent. An investment in yourself!

CHAPTER 49

IMPROVE YOUR ART BY SWIMMING MORE LAPS

Every morning on my drive to work, I see them. Like determined ghosts in the early light of day, they consistently appear. I note not only varying ages and body types but also a shared resolve. Unlike so many voices who lament their weight gain or sluggish energy, these folks are doing something about it. And more importantly, they're doing it consistently.

There's a woman I know who regularly gets up early to go lap swimming. I'm sure she'd rather sleep in. I'll bet the water is brisk. But she swims those laps. She does it for her health, energy, and mental clarity. And she does it consistently.

Not that it's a piece of cake. I've struggled with this consistency thing. Because my workday starts early, I prefer to exercise after work.

My workout usually consists of an evening run with my dog. The next evening consists of weight lifting in my garage gym. Then back to running the next night. But interruptions happen, like city council meetings, social engagements, and such. And the dreaded call of the couch. Maybe if couches were made out of bricks, we'd spend less time on them? Either way, when I fall off the wagon, I lace up those running shoes and dive back in.

The bottom line is that we are what we do. Fit people are fit because they work out regularly. Excellent painters are excellent because they put in the canvas time. Consistently.

Blogger James Clear has written persuasively about the power of changing your habits. His free e-book, *Transform Your Habits*, contains forty-five pages on "how to effortlessly build good habits and break bad ones."

A big part of the equation is using helpful cues to get you started. I mention James Clear because his material was helpful to me (I receive nothing for endorsing his free e-book). But whatever tools you use, the point is to create positive, consistent habits to reach your goals.

The main message of this article is twofold. First, if you want to improve your art, then you need to swim more laps. In other words, you need to put in the time. Tweaking your website, painting what's safe and not pushing yourself will likely bring the same results you're getting now. But if you devote time daily to practice, study, and improve your work, you will see progress.

The second message has to do with exercise itself. Regular exercise seems to improve every aspect of your life. You sleep better, feel better, and perform better. I find regular exercise fuels greater creativity, too.

I often think about my art and writing while I'm running. Ideas come to me as I'm huffing and puffing down backstreets and parks with my dog.

If you want to improve your art, swim more laps. Create a routine of consistent practice and consistent exercise. It doesn't matter where you are health wise. For some, it might be a morning walk. For others, it might involve joining CrossFit. Either way, I think you'll be pleased with the results.

Don't put it off. Even the smallest changes can bring big dividends. Come up with a routine to devote to your art and exercise, and you'll be well on your way!

CHAPTER 50

IF YOU WANT TO SOAR, YOU HAVE TO LEAP

Maybe you are nervous, uncertain, and afraid. Perhaps you're weighing the risks and rewards. Maybe you're not. But you know you want a change. A different outcome. Something inside you persists, pushes, and cajoles until you can't ignore it any more. And so, throwing caution to the wind, you leap.

Like a young eagle who leaves the nest for the first time, you leap. You instinctively know that the comfort of the nest isn't enough. When the fear of staying is greater than the fear of leaving, you leap.

Think back on the accomplishments and breakthroughs in your life. Some may have been due to good fortune and luck. But the most satisfying and meaningful growth often comes from the leap. From the aftermath of charging that cliff and throwing oneself into the abyss.

Diving into the abyss is scary. At first it may feel like you're falling. But then, at some point you experience what the young eagle leaving the nest feels. Exhilaration. Freedom. The thrill of entering a whole new world. New possibilities and dreams.

Country music artist Tim McGraw wouldn't go on stage without a drink. He needed a little "liquid courage" to perform. But it didn't end there. He'd get trashed and "drunk call" his wife. He'd slur. So then, to hide his inebriation, he'd text her. Except everything was misspelled, and she knew. Finally, after one last bender and hangover, he flew into Florida to start a new concert tour. And he decided to quit. He took the leap.

It certainly could not have been easy. The superstar lifestyle is not conducive to sobriety. But he took the leap anyway and never looked back. Today he is in the best shape of his life and more successful than ever.

For me, venturing outside the nest and leaping meant getting on a plane. I had a fear of flying and heights. The fear prevented me from taking trips I should have taken. But then an opportunity came to study landscape painting with renowned artist Scott L. Christensen.

My wife shot down all my excuses about expenses, time away from work, and such. She knew they were sad facades, masking the real issue. My fear of flying.

And so I packed my art gear, stepped on that big plane, and threw caution to the wind. I hated every bump and every time the "fasten seatbelt" light came on. But then we landed, and I felt it. The exhilaration. The joy of conquering my fear.

That turning point led to more painting trips to study with Christensen and significant personal growth as an artist.

What's holding you back? Your weight? An addiction? An unhealthy relationship? Depression? Uncertainty and fear? All of these challenges have real solutions, if you're ready to leave the nest once and for all. If you're ready to take the leap and soar.

Yes, sometimes the flight is bumpy. Sometimes it's the wrong leap, and we fall. And some falls take longer to recover from than others. But playing it safe and never leaping is its own kind of hell.

What a tragedy to not live boldly and pursue your passions. If you want to soar, you have to leap. To that end, I leave you with Theodore Roosevelt's "Man in the Arena" quote:

> It is not the critic who counts; not the man who points out how the strong man stumbles, or where the doer of deeds could have done them better. The credit belongs to the man who is actually in the arena, whose face is marred by dust and sweat and blood; who strives valiantly; who errs, who comes short again and again, because there is no effort without error and shortcoming; but who does actually strive to do the deeds; who knows great enthusiasms, the great devotions; who spends himself in a worthy cause; who at the best knows in the end the triumph of high achievement, and who at the worst, if he fails, at least fails while daring greatly, so that his place shall never be with those cold and timid souls who neither know victory nor defeat.

CHAPTER 51

THE LIFE-CHANGING BENEFITS OF UNPACKING

It's time to open up that old suitcase of yours and do some unpacking. It has sat for years in the attic and collected dust. Perhaps you thought the passage of time and a dark place would settle things? But in reality, before you can move on, you need to consciously let go. Ignoring something and letting go of it are not the same thing. You need to stare it in the face and say "good-bye."

Try this Ann Landers quote on for size: "Some people believe holding on and hanging in there are signs of great strength. However, there are times when it takes much more strength to know when to let go and then do it." How about you? Have you been holding on to something too long? Maybe a bad relationship? An addiction? Regrets? Unrelenting sadness?

Maybe it's time to unpack. Once and for all. Just open that suitcase or trunk and dump the contents out. Like gathering clutter and taking it to the Goodwill, it feels good to let go of stuff. To simplify.

People, places, and beliefs can free us. But they can also imprison us. We must examine each and ask the question: Does this bring me joy?

Marie Kondo, author of *The Life Changing Magic of Tidying Up: The Japanese Art of Decluttering and Organizing*, suggests we use "joy" as the measurement by which we keep or discard possessions. Perhaps the same guideline applies elsewhere in our lives? Such as our relationships, careers, friendships, and discretionary pursuits.

There's a chapter in Dr. Gordon Livingston's book *Too Soon Old, Too Late Smart: Thirty True Things You Need to Know Now*, titled "The Statute of Limitations Has Expired on Most of Our Childhood Traumas." What the good doctor is talking about is mental unpacking. Giving in to the power of acceptance. And then moving on with your life.

Dr. Livingston knows a bit about pain. In a thirteen-month period, he lost his eldest son to suicide and youngest to leukemia. In another chapter of his book, Dr. Livingston teaches that "any relationship is under the control of the person who cares the least." Think about the truth of that one. How many of us have bent over backward trying to please someone who doesn't care so much?

The Stoics understood this stuff pretty well. Men like Seneca, Epictetus, and Marcus Aurelius. In short, their view was that there are things you can change and things you can't. Learn to take action on the things you have control over. Forget about the rest.

You can't change the past. You can't change other people much. Getting to a place of acceptance will free you. It will provide certain clarity. Allow you to step past the anguish and regrets and see the thing as it really is. Once your mental junk is laid bare, it's not so scary. You'll find you can let it go once and for all.

Dr. Livingston has another chapter in his book, titled "We Are What We Do." Amen to that. If you work out every day, then you are a healthy person. If you paint every day, then you are a painter. If you bitch about your life every day, then you are a complainer. You get the idea.

Yes, I know what you're going to say. "It's not that easy. Not that simple."

But it is. You just need courage.

I'm not talking about irresponsibility here. Of course we can't just immediately walk off the job because the boss is a jerk. Or abandon your relationship because it's not bringing you joy. Major changes in your life should be thought out and planned for. Responsibly.

In the end, everyone has to face his or her demons. If you want to maximize the richness in your life, it's best to unpack that mental suitcase sooner rather than later. Accept what you can't change. Focus on what you can. Take action.

If we are what we do, then identify who you want to be. Then start doing the things that person would do. You and you alone must define yourself.

By unpacking all the "junk in your trunk," you can start living the life you always dreamed possible. Imagine what an amazing life it will be.

CHAPTER 52

HOW THE LOVE OF A CAT CONQUERS ALL

Winston awoke to the kiss of sunlight gently warming his arthritic frame. After the recent rains, it felt good to bask in the comfort of morning sunshine. He stirred a bit, testing the rebellion of old limbs and uncooperative muscles. Surely his ninth life had come and gone, and these days were borrowed time. Still, it had been a good run for a cat of mixed breeding and unremarkable roots.

He had known many a cat that faired far worse. Like the Henderson's tabby across the street. Always fixated on those damn squirrels. Yes, the tabby had caught many in his day, until that final chase. Into the street and direct path of a UPS truck. Terrible way to go. Mrs. Henderson shrieked and screamed. And the look on that young UPS driver. Stunned and bereft. But it wasn't his fault. He could never have expected a gray squirrel and old tabby to bolt out in front of him like that. Nope, when your number's up, it's up. Nine lives or not.

Winston elongated and stretched. Gathering steam, he rolled over and wobbled upright. Looking up at the headboard, he saw that she was still sleeping. Good. It had been a long time coming.

After the divorce, she seldom slept much and Winston had worried about her. Many a night he crept up beside the pillow and sweetly nudged her cheek with his wet nose and whiskers. It seemed to stop the tears, and often she'd scoop him up and under the blankets. Then he'd purr, his slow rhythmic vibrations lulling her to sleep. He was most proud of that. Those nights when he could give her quiet comfort.

After she awoke and ambled off to the shower, he made his way to the garage. It was a familiar routine. Litter box. Kibble bowl. Sip of water. Take a nap. What was the sarcastic remark her ex had made? "Cats are worthless. They sleep to eat and eat to sleep." Yep, that's what the jerk said. Which was funny, considering all he ever did was sleep, drink, pretend to work a little, and repeat. Hypocrite.

Winston awoke later on the windowsill in the art studio, to the sounds of soft music. Looking up he watched her humming, sipping a mug of coffee, and painting at the easel. It was so good to see her painting again. He always knew that art would save her in the end. Men may come and go, but cats and creativity were the only reliable companions. The ones you could count on. Yes, she had begun to heal and rediscover herself and her art. There was the beginning of a spring in her step.

In the days that followed, friends started to come over more, and there was laughter in the evenings. Winston would occasionally saunter out into the living room to make an appearance. "Oh, there he is," said one of her best friends, Barbara. "How old is Winston, now?"

And she laughed and answered, "Ancient, but he's been such a good buddy. I couldn't have survived this last year without him." That made Winston feel good. Because he had strived to be there for her. That's what good cats do. Unlike dogs, with their brash affection and predictable slobbering. No, cats communicate their love with reserve and elegance. It's like the difference between a rap song and Bach. No comparison.

The following week it happened. The dull ache in his back had worsened, and finally one morning, he couldn't stand up. He didn't want to alarm her, so he feigned sleepiness when she tried to entice him to get up. After much effort and some pain, Winston struggled to his feet and off the bed. That afternoon he watched her working on a beautiful landscape piece. It had sweeping vistas and mysterious thickets. The kind of environment a cat could get lost in. He closed his eyes and dreamed he was there. In her picture.

Later, he worked hard to edge across the studio and nudge her ankle. She looked down, and he looked up at her. She smiled. "What is it, Winston?" He tried to smile back. Then he looked up at the canvas. He mustered all his strength and hopped up onto the stool. Then he reached out his paw and gently tapped the painting. She looked at him quizzically. "What is it, old guy?" He mewed softly. And then he gazed at the painting. She smiled and ran her fingers through his long mane. "Yeah, I like it too, Winston. It's a peaceful landscape, isn't it?"

"Yes, it is," thought Winston. "So peaceful."

That night, he made his way toward the headboard and purred softly as he nudged her arm. "Do you want under the covers, buddy?" She held open the blanket and pulled him close to her. He could feel her warmth and heartbeat. It was heaven. And it was time.

He closed his eyes and gave thanks that he held out long enough to shepherd her through it all. And to see her paint and laugh and enjoy her friends again. The best part was knowing that she was okay. That she was strong enough now. Capable of weathering the loss of this old fur ball. So he closed his eyes, happily in her arms, and drifted off to what he knew awaited.

She awoke that morning and nudged him. He usually didn't sleep with her all night. He was independent that way. "Come on, sleepy, time to get up." Nothing. She ran her fingers across his back. "How about some warm milk?" But Winston seemed very still. She sat upright. "Oh no, Winston. You can't do this. Winston!" She cradled him close, his whiskers brushing against her face.

And then it happened. Winston twitched. He opened one eye and looked up at her. Then the other eye. "How strange," he thought. "I didn't expect to wake up."

She started to cry and held him close. "Oh, Winston. Oh, Winston." They rocked back and forth together, and Winston felt a bit of hopefulness and energy. Funny how her love could enliven him so. After a wonderfully long time together, she slid out of bed and said, "I'm getting you some warm milk, you old fellow. Because you deserve it. For sticking with me, buddy!" She padded off to the bathroom and then the kitchen.

Winston slowly worked his way over to the window. The sun was peeking through now, and he basked in its healing warmth. "Why stop at nine lives?" he mused. And then she came in with the bowl of warm milk, and he lapped it happily, and she giggled and everything in the world was perfect.

CHAPTER 53

THE GREENHOUSE

They found them in the greenhouse. It wasn't much of a greenhouse, but to them it was a sanctuary. A safe place where she could work with soil and plants while he painted and listened to classical music. Sometimes they'd take a break and have tea outside, at the edge of the lawn where they buried their old dog, Brownie. His death hit them hard, a harbinger for what they both knew lay not far ahead. But then they'd sip their tea and reminisce of the past and New England and their careers and children.

Friends who visited often marveled at how the two had a sort of telepathic connection. Always finishing each other's sentences. "When you've been together as long as we have, well, you just know," she'd say, with that twinkle in her eye.

"And you know when not to say anything. I think that's the key to a good marriage. Keep your mouth shut," he'd retort.

The police received a call from their daughter, who lived four hours away in Springtown. "I'm concerned; they always answer the phone or call back. It's been two days now," she told the dispatcher. And so the patrolmen responded to their old craftsman house on a tree-lined cul-de-sac. They parked on the street and strolled down the nicely kept driveway, lined with closely trimmed hedges. No response at the doorbell, so they went around to the side gate.

"I can see heat coming from the vent," said one of the police officers. "Looks like their furnace is still on." And then he looked closely at the windows, for flies. A telltale sign of death. But nothing was there, just some small potted succulents and two wood-carved figurines.

The officers made their way to the backyard and walked along the footpath beside the lawn. They spied a small cross at the edge of the lawn but had no idea that Brownie, their old collie, was buried there. "Joe, let's check the greenhouse," said one of the officers. They opened the rickety door and slid past some tall, potted ferns. And there they were, seemingly frozen in time. Curled up on the floor against the edge of the greenhouse, with a wool blanket wrapped around them. The old man had his arms around her. Like he was cradling and protecting her.

The officers found no evidence of foul play but were perplexed by the scene. Until they found an envelope sitting atop the old man's French easel. The names Peter and Ashley were written in elegant cursive on the unsealed envelope. For investigative purposes, the officers opened the note and read it.

Dear Peter and Ashley,

Mom and I had a wonderful Sunday in the greenhouse. We enjoyed our tea and then got busy. I worked on my coastal painting, and Mom repotted some lovely peonies. We were reminiscing about the vacation we all took that year to the Grand Canyon and how Brownie got sick in the car. And then Mom gave me this strange look and collapsed.

I held her and said I'd call for help but she whispered no, that it was alright. Then she looked up at me and said she was ready. And we both cried. So I held her for a long time. I grabbed the old wool blanket in the cabinet and wrapped us up in it. I rocked her for a while but knew she was gone. And I guess something inside of me gave up.

I love you both so much. I hope you'll forgive me, but there comes a time in old age when you hear the whispers of your ancestors. And when the love of your life crosses over the vale, well, you feel left behind. If I were younger and my body not so ravaged, I would have stuck around a bit longer. But most days I don't feel so well. I've lived longer than I ever thought. Besides Mom, both of you are the greatest gift a man could ever have. I'm proud of you both and will always be with you. But I don't want Mom to make this journey alone.

So, I'm just going to stay with her now.
All my love,
Dad

The officers stood speechless after reading the letter. They had never witnessed a scene like this before. Heart wrenching and yet beautiful at the same time. Joe, the officer who read the letter, was married. He couldn't help but think about his wife. Later, they called the coroner and police chaplain. The old couple's children were notified, and when reading the letter, they wept and held each other. They later learned that the old couple had their financial affairs worked out and that both children had been provided for.

At the end of his shift, Officer Joe stopped by a florist's shop. When he arrived at home, he found his wife in the kitchen, slicing some bell peppers for the dinner she was preparing. She asked how his day went, but he didn't answer. She turned around to face him, and he handed her the beautiful bouquet of flowers he'd bought. "Oh, Joe, how lovely. Thank you, sweetheart." She kissed him, and he held her close, whispering, "I love you, honey."

She got a vase out of the cupboard and said, "This is the first time you got me peonies. How beautiful." Then she turned to Joe and looked into his moist, glistening eyes. "Is everything all right, honey?" she asked.

"Everything is perfect," Joe said. And then he held her tightly for a long time, not wanting to let her go.

CHAPTER 54

WHY YOU SHOULD DEAL WITH THE BOULDERS BEFORE THE PEBBLES

It is a curious fact that out-of-door nature is to the beginner an enormously overloaded "property room." He sees, for instance, the myriad of leaves upon the tree long before he sees the tree at all.

—*John F. Carlson*

A lot of beginning painters tend to get bogged down in detail. They fasten on a particular area and slave over it endlessly until it's overpainted. Other times, they focus on the one thing that they can do well, to the detriment of everything else.

I remember painting once in a Scott L. Christensen's workshop. I was new to plein air (outdoor) painting. Scott took our entire painting group to a beautiful Idaho vista looking out over the Snake River. Simply breathtaking.

Scott told our group that we had twenty minutes to paint the scene. Then we would be moving on to another location. What ensued was somewhat comical. The more experienced painters set about their work, quickly brushing in the basic shapes and colors of the area. Many of the less experienced painters became a blur of commotion. Juggling their easels and squeezing out paints.

Unfortunately, I was among the newbies. Inexperienced with both my equipment and painting, I fiddled with my gear and scrambled to begin. Looking around, I felt intimidated by how quickly others were working.

I squeezed out my colors, hurried to sketch an outline and begin my painting. Then I spilled my mineral spirits on my palette. And knocked over three brushes into the dirt. Determined, I cleaned up and continued the start of my painting. Which was about the moment Scott Christensen called out "time!" At that point, I was ready to scream.

The group was instructed to pack up their gear, load their cars, and follow him to the next location. And it went like that for half the day.

Needless to say, I learned a valuable lesson about both the organization of my equipment and how to paint quickly. If there is a moral to the story, it would be this: Deal with the boulders before the pebbles. In other words, tackle the big-ticket items first before you focus on the small stuff.

Painter Sergei Bongart said it best: "It is entirely possible, and often advisable, to spend 90% of your time merely adjusting the big, simple shapes before ever moving to the rendering."

Over time, I learned to lay in the big shapes of a painting. I'd paint the outlines of the trees. Block in the foreground and sky. I'd quickly figure out the local color. Not every painter works this way, I realize. Some start with a single object and sort of spiral out from there. But overall, I've found that laying in the big shapes first works well. I also try to quickly determine my darkest and lightest areas. I worry about highlights and details later.

By focusing on the big shapes first, you can sketch in a scene more quickly, and you'll be less fussy. Practice and repetition only improve your speed and ability to craft a sort of shorthand study of a scene. What's more, these quick plein air sketches often result in a sketchy, loose look that many artists find appealing. The work conveys a raw honesty that is frequently more pleasing than a finished, studio piece.

This approach to efficient outdoor painting translates well to other areas of our lives. The author Stephen Covey wrote a bestselling book, titled *The 7 Habits of Highly Effective People*. In the book he describes an exercise where students are asked to fill a jar with large rocks and pebbles.

Many students pour the pebbles in first and then unsuccessfully add the big rocks. Only when they place the big rocks in first and follow up by pouring the pebbles in and around the big rocks, do the students successfully fill the jar. Moral to the story: tackle the big problems first.

In our lives we often get bogged down with the minutia. We fritter with e-mails and small tasks. We procrastinate and avoid the big stuff, which only adds to our stress. But when we finally decide to tackle the big tasks first, we move forward more quickly. And the small tasks are a piece of cake afterward.

Learn to focus on the boulders before the pebbles. Whether it's outdoor painting or challenges in your professional life, tackling the big stuff first will expedite the process, lessen your stress, and get you where you want to go a lot faster.

CHAPTER 55

HOW TO IMPROVE YOUR ART AND PRODUCTIVITY WITH DEEP WORK

Sometimes I fantasize about escaping to the mountains. Staying in some quaint little log cabin with no Internet access. Just a warm fire, food, and the solace of a cool evening breeze dancing across the pines and snow-capped peaks.

I envision the mountain solitude as a perfect elixir for the overstimulation and hurly-burly of modern-day life. A break from the meetings, commitments, e-mails, texts, and social-media superficiality. A place where I can trudge out with my easel and paints, to capture whatever natural beauty inspires me.

I suspect a lot of folks dream about similar escapes. Or a time when things were a bit slower paced and more personally gratifying. As much as today's communication technology enables us to do more, it also imprisons us in an endless digital cycle. I wonder what Henry David Thoreau would say about the world we live in today.

I was up early today and swung by Starbucks before heading to work. Just about everyone there had their noses in smartphones. Often that includes me. Because I get sucked into repetitively checking my e-mails, Facebook, and website activity. We've become so conditioned by the immediate access to information and messages that we forget how to shut all that down and be more in the moment.

This last weekend I read an excellent and thought-provoking book by Cal Newport, who is an assistant professor in the Department of Computer Science at Georgetown University. Cal's book is titled *Deep Work: Rules for Focused Success in a Distracted World*. According to Cal's website, here's an overview about the book:

> Deep work is the ability to focus without distraction on a cognitively demanding task. It's a skill that allows you to quickly master complicated information and produce better results in less time. Deep work will make you better at what you do and provide the sense of true fulfillment that comes from craftsmanship. In short, deep work is like a super power in our increasingly competitive twenty-first century economy. And yet, most people have lost the ability to go deep—spending their days instead in a frantic blur of e-mail and social media, not even realizing there's a better way.

Cal's book taught me about shallow versus deep work. Shallow work is stuff like checking our e-mail and returning messages. Deep work is that undisturbed zone where we are intensely focused and most productive. To accomplish deep work, we need to create routines and habits as well as find places where we can work uninterrupted.

I learned about the 80/20 rule (also known as the Pareto principle), which states that for many events, roughly 80 percent of the effects come from 20 percent of the causes. I discovered how lowbrow activity (watching TV, playing video games, and getting lost in social media) gets in the way of rigorous self-improvement.

If you want to become a better artist and more productive in your life, you need to embrace deep work. That means training yourself to work intensely for longer gaps of time, without interruption. Creating a fixed schedule, learning to say no, and not succumbing to the tyranny of e-mail. Just think how one e-mail can derail your work. Like a request for a meeting date or thoughts on a project.

Time fragmentation happens when we succumb to all these little interruptions. And yet often, these interruptions are not high priority. Cal Newport asks you to consider if Twitter and Facebook are really helping you attain your goals or just distracting you.

You get the point. Consider taking a break from social media or regulating it more. Remember, your calendar and your checkbook say more about how you spend your time than anything. Busy is what happens to you, whereas prioritizing is what you plan to do.

Cultivating a deep work ethic will pay huge dividends on your personal and artistic growth. Imagine setting aside longer, uninterrupted blocks of time to paint, write, or pursue your creative passion. Applying the same approach to your day job will make you more productive in less time.

Consider checking e-mail only in the morning and end of the day. Yes, for some jobs this may not be realistic. But you shouldn't be held hostage to other people's expectation of an immediate response.

Embrace deep work. Limit your social-media addiction. Paint and write more, for longer periods of time. That's what many of the top artists and writers do to achieve more. While the rest of us are counting "likes" and watching cat videos, they're deeply immersed in their painting and writing and creative pursuits. If we do the same, our art and productivity will grow in leaps and bounds!

CHAPTER 56

POSTCARD TO MARY

In your ninetieth year, after a quiet afternoon of flipping through pages in an Irish travel book, you took flight and left us. A silent, peaceful departure as your family tearfully gathered around.

Dad asked you if you were comfortable. You faintly said, "I am." And then, the light faded from your eyes. Dad held a small mirror to your mouth and then declared softly "She's gone."

With your passing came the end of so many treasures. Fresh baked, Irish soda bread. Your soft, lilting laugh. Those gentle hands whose touch always soothed. And most of all, your patience and enduring love of family.

After you left us, I used to wonder, did you book passage on a small detour? Back to the old country of stone fences and rolling hillocks that framed your childhood?

Did you visit the family homestead and neighborhood pubs? The small Irish counties, with their shops and kind people and cheerful ways? Or was the call of long-lost loved ones from a higher realm too strong to resist? Did you forego Ireland and go directly to Edward, your husband, and all who awaited your return?

And so in my fifth decade, I finally made the trip. Back to the lands and people who shaped the kind and loving person you were. Having visited the pubs and people and grand scenery, now I understand. Now I know what your special ingredient was. The leprechaun spirit and Gaelic joy that infused your soul.

Now I understand everything, Mary. Especially how the magic of one's ancestral homeland becomes a part of us. Informing deeply who we are. Much like you can't take the country out of a cowboy, you can't take the Irish out of a lass. It is a part of her, forever.

And so, for a few weeks, I will trace this land over and absorb as much as I can. Attune myself to the distant heartbeat of family ancestors, and fondly remember the angelic grandmother you were.

I am finally in Ireland, Mary! Your homeland, where the rosy cheeks of passersby remind me of you. Where the pubs are full of cheer and music. Where sheep roam the hills and bogs. Where the slower pace of life reminds me that there is more to life than work and social status and needless consumption.

In Ireland I inhale the fresh air of Galway and stand against the fierce breeze of Connemara, whose famous ponies look on from afar.

I lost you, Mary, so many years ago. My kind and loving grandmother. And yet here, upon these magic lands, I feel your spirit again. What strange alchemy that crafts a sense of place. That lives within us, even when we leave our origins and travel to new environs.

My wife and son are with me, Mary. We are traveling Ireland by bus, car, and train. From Dublin to Roundtree. We plan to visit County Kerry, your hometown. I am sharing stories of you as we travel. So that they may know a bit of who you were.

For now, I will close this postcard to you. We have more to take in your honor. But as we continue on our journey, know that you are always with me. Here along the green hills of Ireland. Back in the sun and surf of California. And onward, to the distant shores of time.

Erin go Bragh, Mary, Erin go Bragh!

CHAPTER 57

DO YOU REMEMBER WHO YOU WERE?

My dad used to get up from his reading chair, and I'd watch the whole laborious process. He'd put a bookmark in his novel, set it down, and then lean forward in his chair.

Next, he'd inch toward the end of the chair, put his hands on his knees, and push down on them as he rocked forward and up. A grunt of effort followed as he hoisted his six-foot frame to an upright position. I'd typically make a crack about the rigors of being "an old man." He'd laugh and say, "I can still cut through you!"

Fast forward a lifetime. Dad passed on, and I raised a son of my own. He graduated from high school last month. His nickname for me is "Tom." I asked him once, "Why Tom?"

He flashed a devilish smirk and said, "The old man."

So there you have it. The son becomes a father, and the cycle of life continues. My father is gone now, so I can't compare notes with him. I can't tell him that I get it now. How aging creeps up on us. But also how marriage and raising a child fill our soul with joy.

My teen years were consumed with school, a girlfriend, and competitive tennis. I lettered in high school on the varsity tennis team. I helped teach tennis classes at the community college during the summers.

Back then, I was physically in the prime of my life. Full of energy, passion, and dreams. Tonight I rummaged through a file cabinet in the garage. It's where I keep some of the old family photos. Like this one of my high school tennis years.

Looking at some of the old pictures got me thinking about how much maturity and our professional careers change us. We become more conventional and integrated into the routine of making a living.

We marry, raise our children, pay our mortgages, and schedule vacations. Despite the free spirits who bemoan the notion of "settling," it's not a bad life. I appreciate my home and career and family. I like the stability and security.

But sometimes, the old photos and memories teleport me back. To those carefree summers and days of no responsibility. Back when I used to play keyboards and sing in a rock band. When I played a lot of tennis and had endless energy. And the college years, with all those pubs and parties and time for frivolous pursuits. Those were some good times.

There were the martial arts years. Jujitsu and ninjutsu and sparring with other martial artists. I remember the football player in college who cut in front of me in the cafeteria line. I called him on it, and he called me out. Pride and confidence kicked in.

I followed him outside as a crowd gathered around us. Despite my fear at taking on this muscled opponent, my pride and anger kicked in. Surprisingly, my martial arts abilities kicked in. I easily sidestepped his strikes and tripped him up. He fell into a park bench, and then others stepped in and separated us.

I remember long, easy nights in college when I would spend hours drawing and listening to music. I would also write lyrics and visit the campus music center, where I played the grand piano and sang songs late into the night.

To this day, I play the piano and sing my songs. Because it makes me feel alive and captures the mood of the past. When my hair was long and beer money was always scarce.

Do you remember who you were? Back before life got serious and you had to set aside childish things? Back when the summers lasted forever and everyone you loved was still around, influencing your life?

Do you remember your dreams and hopes and desires for the future? I know these are not necessarily easy questions. Because none of us arrived at exactly where we thought we would. Good or bad, life takes us on detours and unexpected routes. And the good old days weren't necessarily that good for some. But still, most of us were full of dreams and ambitions.

Still, do you remember who you were? Of late, I've ruminated about this. I've been a cop for twenty-six years. No doubt the job and depth of experiences have changed me. Shaped me. I'm more leery of people and cynical than I was in college. But I'm also wiser to the world and its scammers and crooks.

The innocent luster of the world has diminished, yet I can still muster the old enthusiasms. When I slow down and truly immerse myself in who I was, I can't help but smile and get a bit reenthused.

My advice is to take some time to remember who you were. Yes, we've all changed and aged. But our essential selves are still intact. Still there. And if we can plumb those memory banks and call up the old dreams, we might just be able to reignite a few flames. Flames of passion for our art. Or our music. Maybe rekindle a few dormant passions.

After I took my little trip down memory lane tonight, I grabbed a single palette knife and played around with a canvas panel. I scraped and mixed and got lost in the blissful zone of playful creativity.

An Artful Life

I tried to feel a bit like who I used to be. The carefree kid in college, drawing late into the night. Or playing the piano and laughing with friends. Living more in the moment.

The palette knife painting is a bit abstract and unremarkable. But it was fun to just play around and see where it took me. No pressure. No expectations or deadlines or people to please.

Just a quiet evening of oil painting fun. All because I took a bit of time to reflect and remember who I was. And maybe who I still am.

CHAPTER 58

LOVE FROM CHUBBY HUBBY

Carl came to terms with his weight long ago. He knew what it was to be the last kid picked for school sports. Or to have students on the bus slide away from him, because he "smelled." Whatever alchemy of genes and DNA conspired against him, he accepted the result. His life sentence, he used to joke, was to be encased in a bit more padding than everyone else.

Years of dieting and various exercise routines only brought modest results. The weight would go down and then up, just like his spirits. Thankfully, he owned a cherubic face and infectious laugh. Humor was his best friend, and he often deployed it to break the ice and put others at ease. His funny jokes and anecdotes, coupled with his silly laugh and broad smile, usually charmed even the most imperious dispositions.

The school years were rough, but he found his way and garnered a few misfit friends. There was Tyler, a skinny kid with pronounced acne and a stutter. And Grace, whose nerdy glasses and braces camouflaged a sweet soul with an affinity for Jane Austen books. Rounding out Carl's "nerd herd" was Bucky, whose ADHD required some special education assistance. But man could Bucky draw. In fact, in a way, it was Bucky who kind of saved Carl's life.

In his sophomore year, Carl's folks split up. His dad was a binge-drinking alcoholic, and his mom had had enough. So, Dad got an apartment, and Carl lived with Mom. Sometimes he'd hear his mom crying at night, but there was little he could do. He used to tap on her door and say, "It'll be okay, Mom," and she'd open the door and hug him a long time.

Carl knew girls weren't interested in him, so he spent most of his time hanging out with his little crew of friends. One afternoon he was watching Bucky draw some superheroes, and Carl asked, "How did you learn how to draw so good?"

Bucky said, "Mr. Thompson helped me."

Carl had met Mr. Thompson (the high school art teacher) before but never took a class. Carl liked to draw and felt he had ability. So one day he approached Mr. Thompson about taking his art class. The fall of Carl's junior year, he was enrolled in art class. Thanks to Bucky's encouragement and Mr. Thompson's guidance, Carl's life forever changed. For the better.

Emotional pain can shape aspects of your character. Who you become. Sometimes the wounds create a dark heart. Other times the scars imprint a deeper humanity, and your heart holds greater empathy for others. The later was the case for Carl. His imposing mass belied a deep kindness and caring for others. He did not possess a movie-star physique, but he was utterly beautiful on the inside. And sometimes, this kind of beauty is what matters most to others. At least it did for Maddie.

After high school, Carl attended the local state university and majored in art. There he met the incomparable Maddie. With her shock of red hair and Irish heritage, Maddie was a fun-loving and outgoing woman. She saw the depth in people, not merely their exterior. And she loved art.

The two became inseparable, and not long after graduation, they married. Maddie joined a design firm, and Carl turned to fine art. The first few years were challenging, as the art market can be capricious. Still, Carl persevered with his representational landscapes.

One day Maddie found out that Carl's old high school art teacher, Mr. Thompson, was ill with cancer. "You should go see him, Carl," she said. Carl agreed, found Mr. Thompson's phone number, and called. He spoke with Mr. Thompson's wife, who invited Carl to visit. Later that week Carl drove into the Thompson's driveway and to his astonishment, Mr. Thompson was standing at the door, waving.

Over tea and cookies, Carl and Mr. Thompson spoke of the past, high school memories and the world of art. "I always admired the way you took care of your mom, Carl," Mr. Thompson said. He further added, "In the end, it's the ones we love that matter most."

Carl smiled and said, "I know. As much as I struggle with my art career, I always thank God that I have Maddie. She's my rock."

The two talked for hours, and finally Mr. Thompson said this: "Carl, I've looked at your art on your website. You're so close now."

Carl furrowed his brow. "What do you mean?" Carl asked.

"Well, you have all the skills. You've mastered values, edges, composition, and color. You have strong designs in your landscapes."

Mr. Thompson stopped at that and Carl interjected, "But... there's something missing."

Mr. Thompson pulled out a recent art magazine, flipped through the pages, and said, "Look at all this wonderful art. What do you notice?" Carl scanned the images. They were all well-done paintings for the most part. Similar subjects and approaches.

"I'm not sure," Carl said. "I feel like my work is just as accomplished as the work of these other painters."

Mr. Thompson smiled and said, "You're right, and that's the problem."

Mr. Thompson went on to share perhaps the most important lesson that Carl ever received. "Carl," the old art teacher began, "there comes a time when we have to dig deeper. We have to find ourselves. We have to peel away from the rest of the pack. We have to forge our own way and create work unlike everyone else." Mr. Thompson picked up the art magazine again, and he flipped to one particular section.

"Look at these paintings here by T. Allen Lawson. They're close up, long vertical paintings of tree bark. Think about that. Tree bark. No one else is doing that. The paintings are beautifully executed with a muted palette and subtle values. Beautiful and memorable because they're so unique. Or this aerial view painting of chickens. Again, it's different yet beautiful."

Carl felt a wave of excitement. Like he suddenly struck upon the epiphany he'd been waiting for. The key that would unlock the invisible roadblock that had been stalling his career. "You know, Mr. Thompson, I told Maddie that I wasn't sure I wanted to come visit you. I felt bad for not keeping in touch and because of your illness. But she told me that was all nonsense and that I should come see you. She said she thought it was important to."

Mr. Thompson smiled and put his hand on Carl's shoulder. "I'm glad you came, Carl. Your wife was right. Now, do a dying old man a favor. Go back to that studio of yours, and start figuring out what your art is really going to be about. Take everything you've experienced. The joys. The pains. Find that something; and would you start painting that for me?"

Carl teared up a little, wiped below his eye, and said, "Sure thing, Mr. Thompson. Sure thing."

Then Mr. Thompson sat back and said, "And on your way back home, Carl, be sure to pick up a lovely bouquet of flowers. For that beautiful and intelligent wife of yours. I think she did us both a big favor." With that Carl smiled. He could tell Mr. Thompson was tired and that it was time to head back home.

"Thanks again, Mr. Thompson. I'll take your advice. And I want to thank you for all you've done for me."

On his way home, Carl bought that bouquet of flowers. He presented it to his wife the minute he got home. The note with the flowers read, "Be my pumpkin Valentine. Love from chubby hubby." It wasn't Valentine's Day, but Carl was trying to be clever. Maddie loved the flowers and hugged Carl. "So, what did Mr. Thompson tell you, babe?" Maddie asked.

"Oh, to find my voice. March to my own drummer. He gave me a lot to help improve my art. But that's not the most important thing."

Carl smiled as Maddie asked, "Well…what's the most important thing?"

Carl took Maddie in his arms and said, "In the end, it's the ones we love that matter most."

CHAPTER 59

THE ART OF LEAVING THINGS UNDONE

The three of us ran like young gazelles. Leaping and bounding through tall grass into the welcoming woods beyond. With the school year over, the promise of summer was upon us. Warm nights, skinned knees, blue belly lizards, and lunches in the tree house. We were three young friends in the neighborhood. Bonded by age, spirit, and the joy of youthful living.

Each new day brought laughter and adventures. And our furry companions! There was Rosey and Clancy, matching and goofy Irish Setters who often escaped the neighbor's backyard. There was Chrissy, the German shepherd, and Ebony, our dark poodle. There were cats too, but they were largely indifferent to our boyhood exploits. Typical cats.

Dad would come home as the sun was setting. In his suit, carrying his leather briefcase. How foreign to me his world of work, responsibilities, and commitments was. It was not my time yet for adult constraints. My world was an open landscape of dreams, possibilities, play, and carefree living. A time when I could sleep in, except for Saturday morning cartoons. Dad used to tell me, "Enjoy your summer. Too soon the other life will intrude."

Fast forward forty-one years. That ten-year-old boy is now fifty-one. His childhood buddies have long since moved on. Different paths led us apart. Sort of a benevolent drift. The "other life" my father alluded to has indeed intruded.

Adulthood has a way of doing that. It trims away your imagination first. Usually during adolescence, when we start to care less about fantasy and toys and childhood things. When we begin to worry about how we look and what others think. Before long there are relationships, careers, and commitments.

We come home one day to our own children and realize that we are the ones in suits now. Carrying leather briefcases. Exploring open fields and imaginary worlds have become a blur. We turn to new forms of entertainment. Television. Alcohol. Social media. We fill out checklists and establish goals. Objectives. Lose weight. Clean out the attic. Do more. Get ahead.

I remember one Saturday my father sitting on the back patio with a glass of iced tea. There was a gentle breeze, and he was leaning back with his eyes shut. I asked him, "What are you doing, Dad? I thought you were going to hack the weeds on the hillside today?"

He smiled, looked at me, and said, "I'm practicing the fine art of leaving things undone."

Sometimes our souls are worn out. Too much hustle, work, competition, and responsibility. Too much adulthood. Sometimes we just need to leave some things undone. Go run again in the open field. Hike deep into the woods and recapture that youthful spirit.

The art of leaving things undone is not about being irresponsible. It's about taking some time, here and there, to reacquaint ourselves with our childhood. Learning to see the world, for a little while, through our ten-year-old eyes again. They say there comes a time to let go of childish things. But maybe there are times when we should hold fast to them? To regain our sanity, joy, and hope.

An Artful Life

If you're feeling the weight of the world, go ahead and allow yourself this small indulgence. Clear your calendar occasionally, and embrace the art of leaving things undone. All the commitments and urgent stuff will be there when you get back. Just relax; let go of it all, and learn to be in the moment. There is much peace and calm there.

CHAPTER 60

WANT TO IMPROVE YOUR ART AND LIFE? EMBRACE SOLITUDE

The actress Greta Garbo appeared in twenty-eight movies and was a Hollywood icon. She was nominated three times to receive an Academy Award for best actress. Yet, at the ripe old age of thirty-five, she retired from acting and opted for a solitary life.

Garbo neither married nor had children. After retirement, she made no public appearances and tried to avoid publicity. She was known for taking long daily walks, often by herself. She once said, "I never said I want to be alone. I only said I want to be left alone. There is all the difference."

In this day and age of social media, with everyone documenting every facet of their lives, people seeking solitude like Greta Garbo are often viewed suspiciously. Individuals who live alone are sometimes labeled "loners" or "hermitic" and "antisocials."

In reality, solitude can be a very fulfilling way to live. Some people find tremendous peace in solitude. They are able to slow down and savor life on a deeper level. Freed from the burdens of competition, superficiality, and insufficient downtime.

Read *Walden* by Henry David Thoreau, and you'll discover his reason for living alone in the woods:

> I went to the woods because I wished to live deliberately, to front only the essential facts of life, and see if I could not learn what it had to teach, and not, when I came to die, discover that I had not lived. I did not wish to live what was not life, living is so dear; nor did I wish to practise resignation, unless it was quite necessary. I wanted to live deep and suck out all the marrow of life, to live so sturdily and Spartan-like as to put to rout all that was not life, to cut a broad swath and shave close, to drive life into a corner, and reduce it to its lowest terms.

Nature is one of the best places to enjoy solitude and recharge your spirit. Being alone in nature forces you to take in everything around you. There's no cell phone interruptions or conversation to dilute the experience. Getting out alone in nature can be an almost transcendent experience. It's one of the reasons why plein air painters like to get out of their studios.

In Sara Maitland's book *How to Be Alone*, we are reminded of the many benefits and joys of solitude. By spending time with yourself, absent the distractions of TV and smartphones (even books), we rediscover who we are. We become more attuned to nature. Even such simple acts as going for a walk, hike, run, or bike ride can afford you much-needed downtime to enjoy some solitude.

My wife requires downtime in the garden, where she can immerse herself in the peace and solitude of plants, flowers, and soil. When my weekends get eaten up by commitments and I'm unable to go for a run or outdoors to paint, I find I get cranky and off balance. It seems the older I get, the more I'm irritated by the noise of life. Voices on the car radio sound intrusive and harsh. Commercials on television are jarring.

Whether you're an introvert or extrovert, I believe we can all benefit from embracing more solitude. It will quiet your spirit and recharge you. Time outside in nature almost always feeds my creativity. Long walks consistently help produce new ideas and solutions to problems for me. If you're struggling on a creative project, take a break, and get out in nature. You'll return with a different, more relaxed perspective.

Healthy solitude does not mean loneliness. It's simply learning to enjoy being with yourself, slowing down, getting outside, and removing distractions. There's tremendous beauty all around us. Learning to identify different species of birds and their calls can be a refreshing anecdote to fretting over your "likes" on Facebook. Closing your eyes to truly hear the breeze as it kisses the tree leaves above can be exhilarating. It can lead to daydreaming, where we tap our deeper consciousness.

If you want to improve your art and life, learn to embrace a little solitude. The more you do it, the more you'll feel like you can breathe again. The more you'll awaken your creative spirit. You'll honor the memory of Henry David Thoreau, who figured all of this stuff out long before the frenetic, technological zoo we live in today.

CHAPTER 61

WHY AUTUMN IS THE PERFECT TIME TO LET THINGS GO

When Walter hit sixty years, he was drowning. Under water in a sea of clutter, art supplies, papers, broken appliances, old clothes, and unfinished projects. His beloved wife, Alice, died three years ago. After that, Walter became marooned in loss. He started to unravel, feeling unmoored and adrift. Alice had always been his rock. His true north.

Retired many years now from his career as an art teacher at the community college, Walter struggled to make a go of his fine art. He would dutifully amble into his studio, mix colors on his palette, and then stare at the canvas. But nothing would come to him. The muse that used to inform his creativity had taken leave. He wondered if it would ever come back.

The few paintings he did manage to produce were technically well executed but lacked any vitality. Too flat in a predictable, representational sort of way. Saul, owner of the only gallery that sold Walter's work, suggested more color. "Saul, I'm a tonalist. I don't do gaudy, scattershot explosions of color," Walter would say.

"Well, I don't know what to tell you. Something's missing in your work. I mean, the pieces are well done, but there's something not there," Saul lamented.

The missing ingredient in Walter's work was joy. The loss of Alice had stolen a piece of Walter's heart, making him unable to access the happiness he once felt. Worse, the loss of happiness and joy can open the door to fear. And fear, ultimately, was the reason Walter's paintings didn't connect. He was too fearful that if he allowed joy back into his life, it would betray Alice. How dare he feel happiness with Alice gone, he would think to himself.

Autumn arrived and Walter got into the habit of putting on his coat and walking around the local park. The leaves turned striking reds and oranges and rusty yellows. Walter found some measure of solace in his daily walks.

One day Walter encountered a young woman sitting on a park bench, writing in a leather notebook with a fountain pen. It amused Walter that a young person was using a fountain pen, and he struck up a conversation. "Young lady, pardon me, but is that a Parker fountain pen?"

The woman smiled and said, "Why yes, it was my father's. He passed away two years ago of cancer. I love to write my poetry with it."

Walter introduced himself, and the young woman told him her name was Ann. "Really? That was my wife's middle name," Walter said. The two chatted, and Ann told Walter she was a poet. Walter talked about his career as an art teacher and efforts now to sell his paintings. A cool breeze lifted the leaves around the park bench. Walter bowed his head and admitted to Ann that he missed his wife terribly.

Ann put her hand on Walter's shoulder and then looked down at the leaves. She scooped up a handful of leaves, stood up, and faced Walter. And then she said this: "I'll bet it isn't easy for trees to let go of their leaves. I mean, leaves help trees absorb sunlight and water and air. Leaves breathe in carbon dioxide. They produce chlorophyll and make food through photosynthesis."

Walter smiled and said, "Yes, Ann, I'm an old man, but I still remember my grade school biology."

An Artful Life

Ann sat next to Walter, still holding the leaves, and said, "In the fall trees shed their leaves as a way to survive the cold weather. And shedding leaves also helps trees to pollinate in springtime."

"All very fascinating, Ann," Walter said, curious what the biology lesson was all about.

And then Ann dropped the leaves and put both her hands on Walter's shoulders. She looked in his eyes and said, "Walter, autumn is the perfect time to let things go. The people we love and lose would want us to live on. To laugh and cry and even feel joy. There's no betrayal in living and finding happiness again. In fact, doing so honors the ones we loved."

Walter stared at Ann a few moments and then gently began to weep. She hugged him, and for the first time in a long time, Walter felt some kind of weight lifting. A sort of release. He wiped his eyes and told Ann that she was a gift. He thanked her and wished her much success with her poetry. She assured Walter that things would get better. Then she smiled and strolled off into the park, like some sort of wandering angel.

In the weeks that followed, Walter's art took on a new dimension. He began approaching the canvases with a sense of energy and long-repressed hopefulness. He had moved a large photograph of his wife Alice into the studio and found himself gently talking to her as he painted. He imagined that she was pleased with his newfound joy.

Then one day the phone rang. Walter picked it up. "Hello?"

"Walter, I don't know what happened with you, but whatever it is, keep doing it! I've just sold the last of your recent paintings. I'd like to do a one-man show with you this spring. People can't get enough of your work! What's your secret?" Saul asked, excitedly.

"It's autumn, Saul, and someone taught me that autumn is the perfect time to let things go."

CHAPTER 62

AN ARTIST IS A WORLD TRAPPED IN A PERSON

My apologies to the French writer Victor Hugo for modifying his line, "A writer is a world trapped in a person." I was going through one of my old travel notebooks, and there was the Hugo line. I forgot I wrote it down. The more I thought about it, I realized his line would apply to artists, too.

The day I rediscovered the Hugo quote, I was also going through some old paintings I pulled out of a box. As I held the paintings, I was immediately teleported to the place and time I had created them. Some were in the studio, some on location. Between the paintings and the Hugo quote, I realized just how special it is to be a creative person.

Artists, writers, and creative people truly are worlds unto themselves. Within our minds and hearts are so many beautiful things. Past experiences. Vibrant images. Evocative expressions that touch others.

Creative people have the gift of helping others to celebrate the best of the world we live in. Creative people enable others to see things differently.

I still remember some of the children's books I enjoyed as a little boy. They were little worlds that ignited my imagination. I just didn't appreciate the backstory. That it was a creative person who wrote and illustrated those special books.

For all of you who are writers, artists, and creative persons, thank you for what you do. It doesn't matter whether you're famous or obscure. All that matters is that you share your world with the rest of us. Your art helps contribute to a better world.

CHAPTER 63

THERE IS A WAY TO BE BRAVE AGAIN

Nearly two years ago, during the holidays, I encountered a street poet. He was plinking away on a very old typewriter. Selling short poems for whatever patrons felt appropriate.

He typed his poetry on thin, onionskin paper. I remember the distinctive sound of his keys striking the paper. A sound utterly foreign in today's world of laptop keyboards and touch screens.

He was staged just outside a popular downtown bookstore. Location, after all, is everything. Busy, frazzled shoppers couldn't help but stop and take in this intriguing spectacle.

I inquired about his services. He told me there were several clients ahead of me, but if I'd like a personal poem, he asked to leave my name. He suggested I include whatever I was passionate about. So, I wrote down my name and the word "art."

I left to explore the bookstore and shop. An hour later I returned, and the poet told me my poem was done. This is what he wrote:

Advice for Artists—2016—For John P. Weiss

Work.
I am hammering this collection of keys until my fingertips bloom in sores of purple and red:

these, the roses I receive
for the work,
break the spectrum of human experience
of the universal through the prism of self
and do it in pigment,
stretch the paint
until you have built a stair on which
man may climb out
of his lack of kindness;
find this
within you,
it travels on the breeze like a ribbon
in search of a home
and your work
is to give it one
or it will find another more suited servant.

—Kevin Devaney 12-19-15

My favorite line in his poem is "stretch the paint, until you have built a stair on which man may climb out of his lack of kindness."

The poet's name is Kevin Devaney. His WordPress and Tumblr sites state that he "is a graduate of the Sarah Lawrence College MFA program (2011) and a spoken-word advocate. He is the founder of Santa Cruz's only *Weekly Poetry Open Mic*, the *Sarah Lawrence College Spoken Word Collective*, *The Northampton Poetry Brothel*, *Northampton Poetry*, and the former *Art Bar & Cafe Philanthropub*. He is passionate about devising new ways for art to intersect with daily life."

What I admire about Kevin Devaney is his passion and fearlessness. How many of us would be willing to open up a shop on a busy city street, during the holidays, and perform?

How many of us are held back by fear? By that nagging voice in our head, telling us we're not good enough.

The good news is that there is a way to be brave again. All it requires is that you learn to let go.

Let go of the past. Ignore the voices of those who discourage you. They are mired in their own fear and threatened by the ones who set sail.

Let go of your self-doubt and fear of failure. Risk a little to let your true self emerge. Others will appreciate your authenticity and uniqueness.

And should you get knocked down, dust yourself off, and learn from it. Regroup and when you're ready, try again. As Seth Godin says, "Extraordinary benefits accrue to the tiny minority of people who are able to push just a tiny bit longer."

The street poet Kevin Devaney inspired me. He reminded me that creative passion is a gift, if we are willing to be brave, let go of our fear, and share our art with the world.

I hope this holiday season (and beyond), you let go of whatever is holding you back and learn to be brave again. Doing so will enrich your life and probably the lives of many others.

CHAPTER 64

THIS IS HOW TO CONJURE YOUR BEST CREATIVE SELF

Have you ever felt empty? Like whatever magic elixir that used to fuel your creative life just sort of evaporated? That's exactly how Jennifer felt.

She worked at a great design firm in San Francisco. Had a decent apartment and close circle of friends. But her artistic and creative soul felt all used up.

The other day Jennifer was reading an art magazine in a café when she encountered this quote from Gustave Flaubert:

> For a long time now my heart has had its shutters closed, its steps deserted, formerly a tumultuous hotel, but now empty and echoing like a great empty tomb.

Jennifer could relate to Flaubert. Like him, her creative heart felt like a "great empty tomb." Where once she had been full of ideas and artistic yearning, now her energy and enthusiasm for work had waned. She felt adrift.

On her way home from the market recently, Jennifer bumped into Sid. He was a local homeless man with a knack for charming birds. He could often be found in Washington Park charming the parrots of Telegraph Hill. Or feeding the local pigeons.

"I'm so sorry," Jennifer said to Sid. "I didn't see you there when I came around the corner. That's what I get for always rushing!"

"No worries," Sid said. "You should make some time for birds."

"Make time for birds?" Jennifer asked.

"I see a lot of people in this city. Always racing to appointments, in a rush. They think they're busy and getting ahead, but really they haven't learned how to do hard things." Sid reached down to a small cardboard box and opened it up. Inside was a juvenile, white crowned sparrow.

"Why do you have a little bird in a box?" Jennifer asked as she gazed down at her wrist watch.

"Oh, I found him sick in the park, but I've been feeding him and taking care of him. He's almost ready to be on his own again." Sid smiled. "I guess we all have times when we fall down and need to rest before we figure out where we're going next."

"Sid, you said something about learning 'how to do hard things.' What do you mean?" Jennifer wanted to get home, but she was intrigued by this enigmatic bird whisperer.

"Oh, I just mean that people take the easy route. The path of least resistance. Not that they don't work. I mean, sometimes they even kill themselves at work. But they're not doing the hard thing. They're not listening to their heart and pursuing that."

"I guess we all have to make a living before we go find ourselves," Jennifer said.

"Maybe. But our hearts always know when we're living a lie. Do you know what true hell is? It happens when, on the day you die, you meet the person you could have become. If we are to conjure our true selves and our creative best, we need to do hard things. We need to make the changes. Have the courage to walk our true path."

An Artful Life

Jennifer stared into Sid's eyes and nodded. His words struck a deep chord. She realized in that instant that she didn't want to grow old, die, and never become her best self. Her truest self.

The following month Jennifer took a long vacation. She had an MFA in painting and wanted to spend more time at the easel. She drove to Lake Tahoe to visit friends and do some skiing and a little outdoor painting.

One afternoon she drove into the mountains and found a clearing to paint. The air was crisp as she set up her French easel. Everything seemed to be falling into place. The small oil studies she produced were loose and colorful and exciting.

The last several years at the design firm had denied her the time to paint. Her dreams of becoming a fine artist had faded. Until now.

Jennifer knew why she had been feeling empty. She had lost her way. She had fallen down, just like Sid's sick sparrow. She knew now that she would have to do some hard things. Make some changes so that she could pursue the fine arts and follow her dreams.

Just then she felt a flutter of movement beside her. A small bird had landed on her easel. He was eyeing some of the trail mix Jennifer had in a bag behind her easel.

She slowly pinched a bit of trail mix and held it out in her palm. The small bird hopped on her hand and gently began pecking at the trail mix.

"If only Sid could see this," Jennifer thought.

For the first time in several years, a sense of self-assurance and calm washed over her. And she knew. She knew she was on her way to becoming the person she always wanted to be.

CHAPTER 65

WHY GRIT MATTERS MORE THAN GADGETS

We all know people who consistently seem to have the latest, greatest stuff. I can think of one friend who's an Apple junkie. When Apple came out with the iPad, he got one. Same with the Apple watch. If Apple made toothpicks, I'll bet my buddy would buy them.

I was a bit of a paint box junkie. Every time a new paint box (also referred to as "pochade box") came on the market, I had to get one. I resisted a few here and there, but I bought many others. I also made several of my own.

After a while I discovered that the latest, greatest paint box didn't make me a better painter. In fact, I think I wasted a lot of time making paint boxes and checking out new ones online. Time I could have spent painting.

Writer and blogger James Clear wrote about the importance of "grit." He noted the following in his blog post:

> Grit is the perseverance and passion to achieve long-term goals. Sometimes you will hear grit referred to as mental

toughness. Angela Duckworth, a researcher at the University of Pennsylvania, suggests that grit is a strong predictor of success and ability to reach one's goals.

James Clear goes on to note that building strong grit is a lot like building muscle. It's about repetition, habits, and routines. As he wrote:

> Grit isn't about getting an incredible dose of inspiration or courage. It's about building the daily habits that allow you to stick to a schedule and overcome challenges and distractions over and over and over again.

This makes sense to me, and I know it works. Every time I've tried to improve myself or a skill by relying on sheer will power, I didn't fare well. Sooner or later fatigue, laziness, or interruptions would derail my efforts.

The best way to improve and grow is by dedicating yourself to a schedule. James Clear summed it up this way:

> Mentally tough people don't have to be more courageous, more talented, or more intelligent—just more consistent. Grit comes down to your habits. It's about doing the things you know you're supposed to do on a more consistent basis. It's about your dedication to daily practice and your ability to stick to a schedule.

So, purchase that new paint box or popular gadget if you like. There's nothing wrong with enjoying new things. But don't forget that the path to personal growth and creative achievement will only come from hard work and consistency. In other words, grit.

Commit your artistic endeavors and self-improvement goals to a regular schedule. If it's written down and you make it a routine, you'll progress far faster.

The other guy may have a new paint box with satellite reception, but you'll be the one producing better paintings!

CHAPTER 66

WE WASTE A LOT OF IT

I've got a Seneca quote for you.

> It is not that we have a short time to live, but that we waste a lot of it. Life is long enough, and a sufficiently generous amount has been given to us for the highest achievements if it were all well invested. But when it is wasted in heedless luxury and spent on no good activity, we are forced at last by death's final constraint to realize that it has passed away before we knew it was passing. So it is: we are not given a short life but we make it short, and we are not ill-supplied but wasteful of it...Life is long if you know how to use it.

I love that last line: "Life is long if you know how to use it."

How are you using your time? Are you happy with the way you navigate your days? I ask without a shred of judgment because I know I've frittered away my fair share of days.

On my best days, I'm up early and dispense first with the drudgery. The workout, the chores. Then, I hit my stride with an explosion of creative productivity.

I love days like that. Like the afternoon I turned off my cell phone and just painted.

But other days happen. Days when nothing works. The exercise sucks. I'm stiff and unenergetic. The creative output produces crap. Before I know it, it's dinnertime, and the landscape of my day feels like an abject failure.

What I've learned is to not be so hard on myself. We're only human. Our energies and creative expression vary from day to day.

Still, I think Seneca is on to something. After all, he was a Roman philosopher, statesman, dramatist, and tutor/advisor to Emperor Nero. So he kind of knew his stuff.

Seneca was forced to take his own life. Who knows what wisdom he had yet to share? At least, until his fateful end, he used his time wisely. So many years later, we still benefit from his wisdom.

None of us know what our measure will be. All the more reason to take a closer look at how we spend our time.

Remember, "Life is long if you know how to use it." Take a moment to review your calendar, commitments, and habits. Have you crafted a life that allows for the things that matter most to you? Like your family? Your passions?

If not, make some changes. I bet you'll be happy with the results.

CHAPTER 67

THE MORNING FOX

The fox started coming every day after Carole died. It was the strangest thing. One minute we were making buttermilk pancakes in the morning, and then, in an instant, Carole was gone.

She woke me at 3:00 a.m. and said she was having trouble breathing. I fumbled for my cell phone and called. People came, and in a blur I was at the hospital. Bright lights. Noise. Confusion. No one could tell me anything. Finally, they let me in to see her.

"How're you doing, babe?" I held her hand.

"Oh, John. I'm so sorry. I thought we'd have more time. Now, you promise me. Water the flowers in the patio garden. Keep up with your art. It'll keep you sane. And make sure you feed her."

"Feed who?" I asked my beautiful wife. My love. My everything, who was slipping away before my eyes.

"You know who. I named her Eloise, after my grandmother." She leaned back on her pillow, fighting to breathe.

God, I loved her. No one ever prepared me for this. How do you say good-bye to the love of your life?

"Babe, who are you talking about?" I caressed her face.

"The fox, honey. I named her Eloise. Don't you remember? She used to play with Troy." Troy was our German shepherd. He passed away last year. The gentlest dog you'd ever meet. He'd play with all the wildlife. It's like they knew he was harmless. A gentle soul.

"Oh yeah, I'd forgotten. You named her Eloise? That's perfect. She's a beautiful fox. Very elegant and athletic." I looked deeply into Carole's eyes. "This is so hard. I love you so much."

She closed her eyes and grabbed my hand. "Oh, John, this is life. We've had so much. We've been blessed. I'm so sorry we don't have more time. Promise me you'll stick with your art. You do beautiful work. Promise me you'll keep moving people with your creativity. And remember to feed Eloise."

And then she looked at me and said, "Feed her, John. I don't know why, but she's special to me. Feed my little fox."

I told her I would, even though I didn't understand.

Carole fell asleep after that and never woke up. She seemed fine but then cancer can be deceiving. We had a beautiful service, and at the reception, there were many people who talked about my Carole. So many nice things were said. I did my best to be gracious, but I was dying inside.

Death takes a part of us when it steals the ones we love.

I awoke the next day, early. My sleep was fitful, and I felt tired.

Brewed and poured a cup of coffee. Made my way onto the back deck and settled into one of the Adirondacks. The air was crisp, and a breeze washed over my face. It was peaceful.

There was a light dusting of snow on the ground. Everything was pristine and crisp and fresh. And that's when I saw her. She crept out of the brush like a Kabuki theater actor. Stealthily, silently, and with an elegant grace in each footstep. Her tail was full, and her eyes were bright. She was absolutely beautiful.

Just like my Carole.

I remember asking Carole why the fox was so important to her. I mean, there had been other wildlife that visited our home over the years. Rabbits, coyotes, birds, deer. But for some reason the fox touched Carole.

She told me, "I read once about a fox cub that was trapped in a snare for two weeks. He should have died, but he didn't. Do you know why? Because his mother brought him food every day. When he was rescued, he was injured and in pain. But he was also chubby."

I held her hand. "Wow, that's amazing." I smiled at her.

She reached out with her other hand and said, "John, when you go to bed at night, you're going to dream. You're going to be sad and lonely and maybe scared. Just like that fox cub in the trap. But here's the deal. I'm going to come visit you. In your dreams. I'm going to be there for you. Just like that mother fox. I'll take care of you, honey. In your dreams. Don't ever forget that."

I never did forget that. In fact, the morning after Carole's fox came by to visit, I started leaving little treats in the backyard. I dragged the Adirondack chair out to the rear yard. I'd make coffee in the morning and get up early. I'd cook sausage and bacon and take it out with me.

Soon, Carole's fox started coming every morning. Over time, the fox became more comfortable with me. She'd come closer and closer. Sometimes, I could hold the bacon in my hand, and she'd eat it.

Yesterday was Carole's birthday. I got up early and cooked some bacon and sausage for our little fox. But then I fell asleep in the backyard. I was feeling sorry for myself the night before and drank too much wine. So I was a bit hung over and fell asleep in the Adirondack chair.

I've never been a superstitious man or given to religion. But I always sensed that maybe, just maybe, there was more to life than met the eyes. Still, I never dwelled on it.

That early morning of my wife's birthday, as I lay asleep in the rear-yard Adirondack, something amazing happened. I was dreaming, and Carole was facing me. She held my face in her hands, and she told me that everything would be okay. And then she leaned in to kiss me. I felt her soft kiss on my lips.

When I awoke there she was. Eloise. The little red fox. Licking my face. She had eaten the bacon and sausage I left. I guess she wanted to thank me.

Or maybe it was Carole. Maybe she found a way. Through the fox. To reach out and reassure me.

Just like that mother fox who took care of her pup, when he was trapped.

Because I was trapped, too. Trapped in an ocean of grief. Until I awoke with that fox licking my face.

And I knew. I knew everything would be all right.

Now, whenever Eloise visits, I feed her, and we hang out. She's as beautiful as my wife. She brings me peace.

She taught me to be thankful. She helps me understand that Carole will always be with me and that love is the most powerful thing in the universe.

AUTHOR'S NOTE

It's possible for anyone to live a more artful life. Beyond the weekly hours most people devote to their jobs, there's still a lot of discretionary time. The key is to sit down and look at your schedule.

How much of your time goes to television? Social media? Cocktail hour? Clubs or commitments that you could let go? Freeing just one hour a day can make a huge difference in the pursuit of your passion.

Everyone's lives are unique, and we're all in different seasons. Some are in school, starting out. Others are raising children or immersed in their careers. Some have retired. The good news is that whatever the season, you can make room for your artful endeavors.

There will be setbacks, illnesses, and unexpected events. But crafting a schedule that makes time for your creative passion will feed your soul and lead to more artful living. You owe it to yourself to give voice to your creative expression.

I wish you every success.

Visit me at JohnPWeiss.com for the latest artwork, articles, and cartoons.

SPECIAL OFFER

Clint Watson and the gang at FASO have a special offer for readers who want to create their own professional-artist website. Whether you're just starting out or moving content from another website, FASO has you covered.

Sign up today with FASO using this special link, **http://faso.com/ref/47118** to get your first month of service and hosting for free!

FASO is the preferred online platform for artists who require a professional website. FASO websites include blog and newsletter features, are responsive (which means they look good on large screens, laptops, and mobile devices), and have superior support.

FASO is the only website platform I trust to share my fine art. Come join the FASO community today!

ABOUT THE AUTHOR

John P. Weiss is a writer, painter, cartoonist, and former chief of police with over twenty-six years of law enforcement experience. He was a one-time student of American painting icon Scott L. Christensen, and his cartoons have been featured in past issues of Charles Brooks's *Best Editorial Cartoons of the Year*. Weiss has assumed more than a few job titles in his life, and *An Artful Life* is the literary summation of his many talents. He currently lives in southern Nevada with his wife, son, and two dogs.

Made in United States
Cleveland, OH
11 January 2025